The *new*
New

The he new New

Edited by Ulrich Dietz

Leading intellectual forces from culture, business, science, and art on a new way of thinking as an opportunity for the future.

Contents

Prologue

Conversations

44

52

68

78

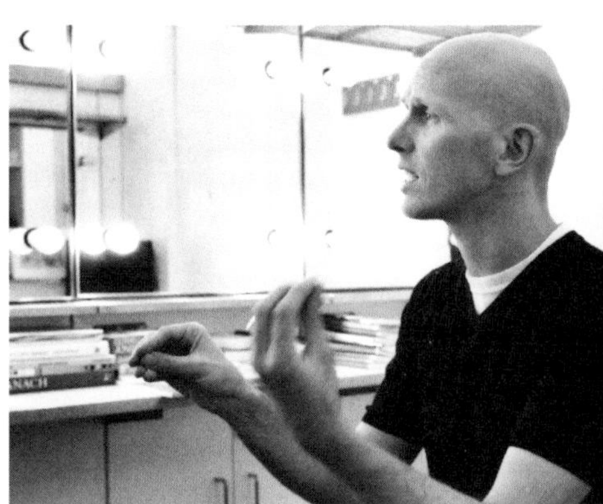

94

102

118
126

142

152

168

176

Albert Einstein

"If at first an idea
is not absurd, there is
no hope for it."

At its core, the new is paradoxical. It is there, but most people do not perceive it, neither in themselves nor in others. They distrust ideas that sound strange or outlandish, and by doing so they nip every kind of innovation in the bud. New ideas mostly do not yet have a form, much less a familiar one; that is why they are frightening at first. As an IT entrepreneur, I constantly have to deal with new technologies, products, and markets, if only because of my profession. To preserve our success and remain globally competitive, we have to constantly find and invent the new. We Germans are without a doubt a nation of inventors. Every other nation is too, but our spectrum is astonishingly broad.

The pioneers who confronted the "venture of creation" (Georg Christoph Lichtenberg) revolutionized the world. For example, the chemist Felix Hoffmann, who invented aspirin for Bayer in 1897; other trailblazing thinkers include Johannes Gutenberg and Konrad Zuse. To the former we owe, as everyone knows, movable type printing since 1440 and to the latter, precisely five centuries later, since 1941, the computer. Jeans were also dreamt up by a German in 1873: the emigrant Levi Strauss; much later, in 1953, Adolf Dassler, the founder of Adidas, produced the first athletic shoes.

"Made in Germany" is still considered a sign of quality for high-quality products. In some sectors, German companies still lead the way, such as in energy and medical technology. At the same time, in Germany as all around the globe, many companies and fields of activity continue to be subject to inertia. Fear of risk causes managers and employees alike to cling to paralyzing habits, to water necessary changes down with compromises, and to look backward rather than forward.

A listless status quo at the cost of an urge to explore threatens the future prospects of the global society at the beginning of the millennium. What we urgently need is a worldwide network for a culture of discoverers, who thrive best in ideas workshops. The remarkable TED Conference (Technology, Entertainment, Design), which was founded by the architect and graphic designer Richard Saul Wurman in California in 1984 was initially such a small, even somewhat chaotic laboratory.

Its motto "ideas worth spreading," was the initial spark for the book *The* new *New*. Together with my team, I wanted to meet people from a wide variety of fields who were linked by one thing: their drive to go beyond the already existing and to abandon comfortable securities for passionate convictions. What they all have in common apart from that is their pronounced individualism and their independent, self-willed thinking. Both these qualities, which are interdependent, have enabled them to follow their dreams, ideas, and goals unwaveringly despite all obstacles. Each of these visionaries, pioneers, discoverers, and founders began on his or her path with small, tentative steps. Years of tough, hard work with many setbacks followed, during which they gradually transformed an insight, a stroke of genius, or a big bang event into a product or work that simplified our common lives or made them more healthy, more beautiful, or simply better. They never achieved this acting alone. Innovations are always indebted to idealistic comrades-in-arms who believe in something just as unshakably. When the new prevails in the end and develops its effect, a circle of positive feedback results for all involved and sometimes for millions of others as well.

"People who make new things despite all the resistance are precious. They ensure society's survival," says media theorist Peter Weibel. The interview with him was just as enriching and encouraging as the conversations with our seventeen other partners. Each of these great entrepreneurs, scientists, researchers, and artists conveyed to us in his or her own way that it is not impossible to be innovative. So get started!

Ulrich Dietz

Carole Cadwalladr

"Ideas are the
new rock 'n' roll."

What does the future of the new look like? The film *Inception* by the British-American director Christopher Nolan, starring Leonardo DiCaprio and Marion Cotillard, is about how ideas come about in the post-metaphysical era of the present. The source there is no longer freely floating inspiration but rather inception, a controlled process with which ideas are implanted in people and then calculated to be turned into innovation with the aid of professional seminars and special training sessions.

Is that what the future of the new will look like? No. Ideas cannot be shifted at will from one head to another to be cultivated to innovative maturity there, made interchangeable, as it were. Ideas are as original as the personalities who have them, even when they are in the air and several people with sensitive antennae pick them up at the same time.

But only the person who transforms them into deeds and facts is an inventor, and only the one who makes them marketable is an entrepreneur like the American Thomas Alva Edison was, to whom we owe not only the lightbulb and electrification but also dozens of sayings on the subject that are as insightful as they are quick-witted. He was a genius who started from nowhere, and so he knew: "A 'genius' is

often merely a talented person who has done all of his or her home-
work," but also: "Genius is 1 percent inspiration, 99 percent perspiration."

How true: "No pain, no gain." You do not have to be a genius to notice
quickly, as I did as a young engineer, that "a magic is inherent in every
beginning," as the writer and poet Hermann Hesse incomparably
expressed it. But inspiring enthusiasm alone cannot solve the problems
that come up over the short or long term; you have to roll up your
sleeves. For, as Edison put it, "there is no substitute for hard work."

At some point in all the interviews conducted for *The* new *New* we arrived at this place, the foundation that even the tallest tower requires.
But what are the innovative elements that go beyond a determined will
to do something?

Each of our interview partners embodies it with different nuances and
facets. Whereas in the case of Anousheh Ansari, the space traveler,
it is the talent to approach a utopia by way of a childhood dream, in the
case of the physicist Lisa Randall it is the urge to explore paired with
the talent of vision. The artist Tobias Rehberger is creative because
with everything he encounters he asks if it could not also function

completely differently, and the media theorist Peter Weibel needs only a little data to grasp a situation long before others do.

The design manufacturer Alasdhair Willis analytically decodes the essence of brands, and designs his own from that. René Redzepi, the world's greatest chef, and the jewelry manufacturer Roberto Stern redefine luxury by reflecting on their roots.

The architect Ken Yeang and the economist Antonella Battaglini are avant-gardists of a green aesthetic because they network nature and technology to new eco infrastructures. The auto designer Murat Günak and the underwater vehicle engineer Graham Hawkes boldly dropped out of promising careers to pursue their own imagination and develop vehicles for a decelerated future. The investor Paulus Neef and the pharmaceuticals entrepreneur Edwin Kohl unwaveringly followed their founder's instinct, and the economist Amar Bhidé swam against the tide by linking consumerism and innovation.

The philosopher Susan Neiman developed a revolutionary moral doctrine for the third millennium from Kant's categorical imperative, while the director Claudia Llosa developed an equally radical visual language for the power of empathy. The anthropologist and discoverer Josh Bernstein and the choreographer Wayne McGregor charismatically open up for their audiences unexpected landscapes and physical languages.

These eighteen trailblazers will certainly not be the only ones who contribute something to the future of the new. There are many other renowned innovators around the world. I made my selection because these personalities and their stories fascinated me especially.

Countless people are currently brooding on, fiddling with, tinkering on, researching, and experimenting with shaping the present. Their ideas are their precious raw material; networks and platforms are their marketplaces of ideas. This boundless potential will result in the rock 'n' roll of our future.

Anousheh Ansari

"Our nature
itself is the origin
of the new."

Anousheh Ansari

She demonstrates how one can become successful by dreaming. Born in Mashhad, Iran, in 1966, the entrepreneur is the first woman to travel to space in a Soviet Soyuz spacecraft, at her own expense in 2006. Conquering the universe and the starry sky had been her passion since childhood, and after studying electrical engineering and computer science, she worked hard to achieve it. With her husband and brother-in-law, Anousheh Ansari cofounded the electronics company tti, which they sold at the turn of the millennium for 550 million dollar and shortly thereafter established the holding company Prodea. With it she financed, among other things, the generous Ansari X Prize to support the private development of space flight. Ansari's recently published book, *My Dream of Stars*, is also concerned with bringing Earth a little closer to the cosmos.

She is once again pursuing her greatest mission: promoting the fact that the paradise of the heavens is close enough for anyone at any time to touch. This is our good fortune, since it means we have an opportunity to meet the space traveler in one of the most noble hotels in Amsterdam, the Pulitzer, located on the picturesque Prinsengracht. It is still very early, but the Iranian-born entrepreneur looks stunning and as fresh as the morning dew. As we enjoy coffee, croissants, and lots of water in the garden, she describes in her gentle voice why she found the universe irresistibly attractive even as a child, and how much she took on, both financially and physically, to that end. She is a thoroughly feminine, powerful woman, who would like to be an example for others. Given her force of will, it is easy to picture this charming enthusiast simultaneously running yet another successful company.

Ulrich Dietz In 2006 you were the first female private astronaut to travel to the ISS (International Space Station) in a Soyuz TMA-9 spacecraft, together with the American astronaut Michael Lopez-Alegria and the Russian cosmonaut Mikhail Tyurin. You paid around twenty million dollars. Was your desire to escape the earth so great?

Anousheh Ansari Oh no, this was not about escaping earth but about experiencing space. I finally fulfilled my biggest dream, which I have had since early childhood. In 2001 when I saw news images of Dennis Tito, an American businessman and former space engineer who was the first private individual to fly into space, I thought: one day I will do that too. In 2006, just like Tito, I was able to join the Russian space program to fly with a Soyuz to the ISS.

Ulrich Dietz Five years later, you were realizing your dream.

Anousheh Ansari I am the best example of how dream becomes reality. It is not the realists but the idealists, enthusiasts, dreamers, and visionaries who are the true innovators. These are the people who can use their imagination and dream what is "not," and make it come true.

Ulrich Dietz Having a dream as an initial spark is one thing, I'll grant you that. But that alone does not produce the capital that makes a space flight possible.

Anousheh Ansari That's true. In 1993 I cofounded tti (telecom technologies incorporated) along with my husband, Hamid, and my brother-in-law, Amir Ansari. Our company was small from the beginning, and we had little money. But I worked passionately and very hard to ensure it grew. In fact, we were able to sell tti at precisely the turn of the millennium to Sonus Networks for 550 million dollars. We had extraordinary luck, because the bubble burst right after that.

Ulrich Dietz What did you study?

Anousheh Ansari Electrical engineering and computer science like my husband, my sister, and my brother-in-law. We are a family company and work together day and night.

Ulrich Dietz It is a privilege to be able to spend so much time with those closest to you. There is even a prize named after your family. What is the Ansari X Prize?

Anousheh Ansari X Prize is a foundation established by Peter Diamandis. He is also obsessed with space like I am. His idea was inspired by the Orteig aviation prize that was won by Charles Lindbergh in 1927 and wanted to use competition to change the paradigm in space travel to find solutions for supposedly insoluble problems by offering corresponding prizes for pioneers in all disciplines. Diamandis wants to launch a new kind of competition that is no longer about making a profit for oneself but about benefiting everyone.

Ulrich Dietz I share your passion. You endowed the Ansari X Prize with ten million dollars. Why?

Anousheh Ansari Opening up the space frontier for every one requires risk and large investment, something that only an entrepreneur would do, not government agencies. That was X Prize's goal. In 2004, around the forty-third anniversary of Alan Shepard's suborbital flight in space, Burt Rutan's SpaceShipOne took its first flight. He is an aeronautical engineer and the founder of Scaled Composites, a company that develops aircraft prototypes. This was the first privately funded space flight ever. It completely changed the game.

Ulrich Dietz Rutan is a great visionary and brilliant design engineer. He also designed SpaceShipOne. It is the first private airplane with rocket power, which achieved an altitude of more than a hundred kilometers and thus entered space.

Anousheh Ansari That's what he won the prize for. Paul Allen, the cofounder of Microsoft, funded the operation to construct it. Everyone involved was taking a big risk, since at the time there was no privately funded manned space flight program. There was nothing and no one supporting such projects. It only started after our prize. After the Prize was won, Richard Branson purchased the design for SpaceShipOne and built SpaceShipTwo with Rutan.

Ulrich Dietz In March 2010 the space capsule just made its maiden flight. If it begins regular take-offs in 2012 as planned, I will be one of the first on board. Tell me about your experience in the universe: What did you feel sitting on top of a rocket being shot into the universe at supersonic speed?

Anousheh Ansari During the flight we were buckled in and couldn't see anything. But once we were in a safe orbit, we could finally get out of our seat and see Earth from space through a window…That was certainly the most emotional moment I have ever experienced! Seeing this sublime, infinite space with your own eyes is an experience no photograph or video can replace. Such incredible images leave an indelible impression. It's like stepping out of your body. You see your whole life below you in a sense: your house, your family, your memories. I cried. It was so incredibly moving. Of a previously unknown beauty that triggered something in my innermost soul.

Ulrich Dietz You can't have the same experience in a passenger jet. I flew on the Concorde several times and can at least imagine what you mean. You are at an altitude of twenty thousand meters and can see Earth's curvature a little. How did you experience the speed?

Anousheh Ansari I was surprised by how smooth the flight was, hardly rougher than an airplane. Except the pressure was higher than in a normal plane. But the flight back to Earth is much more difficult. You get shaken up; there are hard bumps; you feel quite powerfully the reentry into the atmosphere. Through my window I saw flashes of fire; it was dramatic. I felt like a shooting star.

Ulrich Dietz Were you afraid?

Anousheh Ansari No. I had expected to flip out entirely, but my pulse remained calm. It certainly helped that I had prepared for six months in a simulator, with meditation, among other things. Up to the second when the engines started, I felt I was in a surreal fairy tale.

Ulrich Dietz And the outdated Soviet technology didn't worry you?

Anousheh Ansari It's true; it was somewhat antiquated, but it works!

Ulrich Dietz How demanding was the training?

Anousheh Ansari Very. Finally, it is preparing the body to an incredible challenge, because it has to totally adjust in space. For the first few days, you are violently sick; all of the blood is running into your head; your face swells up because you are exposed to such pressure. I had bad headaches and my spine lengthened; I got about two inches taller. Unfortunately, you loose them again when you return, and instead your coccyx hurts quite badly for several days.

Ulrich Dietz That sounds like an extreme experience. Not everybody will withstand it.

Anousheh Ansari Yes they will. Any healthy person can do it, so long as he or she doesn't stay up there too long. For me, it was eleven days, but some astronauts spend as much as half a year in space. That has a much stronger impact on the body. Your muscles begin to atrophy and bone density decreases, even if you do strength training for two hours a day, as all the astronauts do. That's because the body gets lazy in a weightless state. Down here, we are not even aware how much energy we have to use just to lift a glass of water. In the spaceship you learn to be very careful with things.

Ulrich Dietz During your flight, you studied, among other things, radiation intensity; you did blood analysis and researched your muscle mass.

Anousheh Ansari Right, I was a volunteer guinea pig.

Ulrich Dietz It is astonishing what some people will do to realize their dreams.

Anousheh Ansari Yes. As long as people dream of the impossible, whether physically, mentally, or psychologically and use the imagination we are built with. Then our nature itself will be the origin of the new.

Ulrich Dietz Can innovation result from passion?

Anousheh Ansari Absolutely. Let's take long duration space mission for example; one idea would be to recruit people who are paraplegic to be the new astronauts.

Ulrich Dietz Who would come up with such a bizarre idea?

Anousheh Ansari Well, it sounds horrible, but for long journeys in space, people with such a disability would make the best astronauts, and they don't have to worry about damage to their muscle. On the other hand they would be able to move — I should actually say fly which is something they could never do in the gravity of our planet.

Ulrich Dietz Would you go that far?

Anousheh Ansari If someone were to offer me a ticket for a very risky flight into space, for a mission from which I would probably not return, I would accept it!

Ulrich Dietz What do you find so extraordinarily fascinating about it?

Anousheh Ansari Even I find it difficult to explain. Perhaps I am a creature from another star who wants to get back. Seriously, though, space has always been my greatest obsession. I devote every free minute to cosmology and the origin and meaning of our existence. My love of science is coupled with a desire to find a response to what makes our life essential.

Ulrich Dietz Did you find it by getting closer to the stars?

Anousheh Ansari Yes. It was a revelation to realize that there is something so much larger than you. Up there the stars shine with an unbelievable intensity; the sky is covered with them. I have always believed that there are other creatures and other dimensions. Why should we be the only ones? Especially when our lifespan is at most a blink of an eye when compared to that of space.

Ulrich Dietz Lisa Randall, the physicist in our book, works on multiverses. Do you also believe in them?

Anousheh Ansari Yes. I'm crazy about astrophysics, string theory, and speculations about hidden dimensions. Nor can I accept that the speed of light is the fastest speed at which we can move. That can only be a cosmic joke! The universe is so large; we cannot be bound only to our solar system!

Ulrich Dietz Are you a spiritual person?

Anousheh Ansari Yes I am. I believe in transcendence, that there is a power the universe created and that is contained in everything. We too are part of it and are connected to one another through it.

Ulrich Dietz Back to earth. Is your adopted country, America, still the motherland of the pioneer spirit as far as research and entrepreneurship are concerned? Or are guiding intellectual forces now found more in Europe, India, or Iran?

Anousheh Ansari Innovative scientists have always been found everywhere, in America as well as in Europe, the Middle East, and India. But the people in some countries do not yet have the education, the opportunities and experience of the West. But they are learning.

Ulrich Dietz What is the situation in your native country, Iran?

Anousheh Ansari We Iranians are born entrepreneurs, but we still have too little training in management standards. Though I founded my company with no knowledge in the field and only later took a couple of finance courses.

Ulrich Dietz I never attended a management school either, but it can't hurt to study additional tactics at a business school and to start to build a network early. Do you see yourself as a role model for women from the Middle East?

Anousheh Ansari I hope I am, and it makes me very proud. I really want to encourage all women to believe they can achieve what they have set out to do. We women should learn that our strengths are those that separate us from men, not those we share with them. Our own view of things is our capital; that is the foundation of our power!

Ulrich Dietz Was your education liberal?

Anousheh Ansari Yes. My father worked in sales and marketing; my mother worked in university administration. Our parents always spurred us children to study. That is really typical of our country; we consider education very important. That is why there are so many very well-educated young people in Iran, especially women. 60 percent of the university students are women.

Ulrich Dietz A large number, but do women have a professional future after university?

Anousheh Ansari That's the problem. Ordinarily, this potential intelligence would be our future; 75 percent of the population is under twenty-five. But with this economic situation and lack of opportunity in the country…It's a time bomb.

Ulrich Dietz Do you have a different view of NASA's space flight program since your expedition?

Anousheh Ansari If the last space shuttle is retired in early 2011, as planned, the United States will not longer have its own spaceshuttle to fly to the ISS. The planned successor model, the Ares/Orion, will not be ready before 2015, and its future is uncertain because of the financial crisis.

Ulrich Dietz That only improves the odds for privately funded space travel, which President Barack Obama is seeking as well. But won't it be a few years still before space flight is affordable for average earners?

Anousheh Ansari Probably. Fortunately, there are more and more sponsors and investors such as Elon Musk. In 2002, he founded the company SpaceX, which specializes in commercial space travel; its goal is to transport satellites and other freight into space as cheaply as possible. In the end, he wants to be the first to get to Mars in a rocket. He has already taken an important step in his master plan, since his carrier rocket Falcon 9 made its first successful test flight into space in June.

Ulrich Dietz Musk is a genuine entrepreneur who is interested in making complicated products inexpensive and suitable to the masses. As early as 2003, he invested in Tesla Motors, a manufacturer of electric cars that recently went public. He also founded SolarCity, a company that produces and installs solar power plants. But won't Mars continue to be a utopia for a while?

Anousheh Ansari It seems so. It takes more than a year to travel there and back; no one knows what effects it would have on the psyche. Radiation is another important risk factor.

Ulrich Dietz As an ambassador for privately financed space travel, what would you want to say to interested lay people?

Anousheh Ansari Above all, I want to get as many people as possible excited about discovering the universe with their own eyes. Then they will better understand how precious Earth is; they will work harder for sustainable and socially minded solutions and they will understand that we only have one home and that unless we learn to live together peacefully we will all lose. They will better understand that progress in space technology benefits other areas of research as well which make our lives better here on earth. Last but not least, the prices will fall if space tourism becomes more popular.

Ulrich Dietz Do you love Earth more or less since you have been in space?

Anousheh Ansari More. When I saw it from above, in all its diversity and beauty, I thought: it's still the only place we will be able to survive over the long term. It became irrefutably clear to me that our planet itself is the most sublime vision we could ever have.

Antonella Battaglini

"We have to transcend our mental limits, otherwise we will have no future."

PIK
POTSDAM-INSTITUT FÜR
KLIMAFOLGENFORSCHUNG e.V.
Michelsonhaus A 31

Antonella Battaglini

In the mid-1990s she moved from Italy to Germany for love. Born in Rome in 1963, she studied business management and was a manager in the pharmaceuticals industry before beginning a new career in Germany. At the Potsdam-Institut für Klimafolgenforschung, she has devoted herself to renewable energies since 2001. The concept that she introduced to the public in 2007 was pioneering: the SuperSmart Grid. It is a super intelligent electricity grid that will combine the transmission grids of the future to bring electricity from wind, biomass, and solar power around the globe as needed. In the meantime, Battaglini continues to pursue her vision in another way: with the nonprofit organization TheCompensators* she purchases emissions allowances from the European emissions trade and eliminates them.

Not everyone has the privilege to work in a building as steeped in history as the former astrophysical observatory that now houses the Potsdam institute for climate impact research on the Telegraphenberg in southwest Potsdam. Beginning in 1874, the architect and senior planning director Paul Emanuel Spieker embedded the clinker buildings and majestically domed observatories into an English garden. Presumably it did as much good for the scientific geniuses doing research there around the turn of the century—above all Albert Einstein—as it does Antonella Battaglini now. Our conversation takes place in a rather sober seminar room, but afterward the dainty economist takes us through the spacious building and up to the grand room beneath the dome. Beneath the wood-paneled vaulted ceiling is the great refractor, an architectural landmark and the fourth largest lens telescope in the world, dedicated in 1899 by Kaiser Wilhelm II himself. Unforgettable —as is the panorama view from the balcony.

Ulrich Dietz You work on the Telegraphenberg in Potsdam in a very beautiful historical building.

Antonella Battaglini You mean our main building, the former astrophysical observatory. In 1915, the then director Karl Schwarzschild discovered here the first exact solution to the field equations of Albert Einstein's general theory of relativity. Einstein himself worked here on various research projects in the 1920s, which is why the science park in which our main building is located is named after him. This park also has Erich Mendelsohn's famous Einstein Tower, a solar observatory. Our neighbor in the park, the Geoforschungszentrum (Geo research center), became famous after the seaquake in the Indian Ocean in 2004, which caused a catastrophic tsunami, and it was commissioned to develop a new early warning system for tsunamis. Because the PIK has grown a lot recently, my office is no longer on the Telegraphenberg but on the northern edge of Potsdam.

Ulrich Dietz How long has the Potsdam-Institut für Klimafolgenforschung (PIK; Potsdam institute for climate impact research) been in existence?

Antonella Battaglini It was founded in 1992, and its director since that time has been the physicist Hans Joachim Schellnhuber. I came to the institute in 2001, and since then I have been working in the field of renewable energy. Originally, I studied business management and was a manager in the pharmaceuticals industry for ten years. As an outsider, I could see that there were both reasonable and less reasonable approaches in the area of climate policies.

Ulrich Dietz Did you find that coming into it from a different career made it easier to come up with new concepts?

Antonella Battaglini Certainly! Precisely because I am not from the field, I could come up with new ideas such as the SuperSmart Grid. Many experts are so close to the solution of a problem that they no longer see it.

Ulrich Dietz The SuperSmart Grid. There is already the SuperGrid and also the so-called Smart Grids as well as No Grids. You combined the first two. How should we imagine it?

Antonella Battaglini Let me return to the beginning of energy sources, to the era of fire and candles. Later there was oil and gas, and with electrification systems emerged the conditions that initially generated electricity only for their immediate surroundings, but soon electrical energy was being transported over ever greater distances. The number of power plants increased rapidly, and in the 1930s the electricity companies formed the first monopolies. Today, as a consequence of globalization and climate change, we have reached a point where everyone in the world has to be as thrifty and environmentally friendly as possible with energy sources. Sources of renewable energy have been discussed for many years but they have never been as much in vogue as they are now. Why? Because of the greenhouse effect, which, as we all know, is caused by extreme quantities of carbon dioxide in the air that is being released by human activity. This greenhouse gas output has to be radically reduced in order to limit global warming to two degrees Celsius.

Ulrich Dietz With your SuperSmart Grid, you want to produce 100 percent of the electricity from renewable sources. Isn't that an audacious assertion?

Antonella Battaglini I watched for a while as the increasingly numerous advocates of renewable energy became more and more aggressive toward one another. They fought over one percent of renewable energy, more or less, rather than understanding that in order to begin using renewable energy on a large scale in a timely manner we need a number of different approaches and technologies. By combining various technologies, each of which has its specific strengths and weaknesses, we can indeed produce 100 percent of our electricity from renewable energies at acceptable costs.

Ulrich Dietz This observation was your initial spark. But how does it look with the current energy scenario? Can you give us a brief overview?

Antonella Battaglini Currently, Europe is producing about 15 percent of its electricity needs from renewable sources, with several countries, such as Germany and Denmark, leading the way. Thus far, most of the growth has come from wind power. In southern Europe, especially in Spain, it is primarily solar energy. That is very important because this technology is ideal for the earth's sun belt, obviously including North Africa. At the same time, decentralized energy production has been making progress with the development of so-called virtual power plants. One famous advocate of decentralized energy is the Social Democratic politician Hermann Scheer. Recently the International Renewable Energy Agency (IRENA) was founded by 142 states.

Ulrich Dietz Didn't the North-South Commission under Willy Brandt make the first proposal for such an agency as early as 1980?

Antonella Battaglini Right. In the meantime, however, the world has clearly continued to develop. Until recently, most people thought that we had to decide between central—that is, large—technology and decentralized electricity generation. But now we know that both approaches can and must be combined. That is what my team and I have developed with the SuperSmart Grid.

Ulrich Dietz What are Smart Grids?

Antonella Battaglini Currently, Smart Grids are the intelligent grids of the future. They are supposed to take electricity produced locally in a decentralized way and distribute it to order as needed. They regulate energy production and use it more efficiently and hence more cheaply. The truly brilliant thing about them, though, is that electrical networks and communication equipment is intelligently networked so that, for example, your washing machine is informed by the electricity company about excess electricity in the network and can use it cheaply.

Ulrich Dietz And Super Grids?

Antonella Battaglini Super Grids are transmission networks that take electricity from renewable sources—wind, biomass, solar, thermal—and transport it across great distances with little loss. With their help, electricity can be produced where renewable energies are plentiful and hence cheap. This electricity can then be brought to where it is needed. Fluctuations in production—the big problem with renewable energy—are largely evened out by production over a large area. The remaining fluctuations are stored using pumped storage hydroelectric plants and biomass power plants. One challenge results from the bottlenecks of cross-border transmission lines.

Ulrich Dietz This technology is comparable to so-called Cloud Computing.

Antonella Battaglini You are referring to networks of computers in computer centers that can be accessed via the Internet, which are intended to replace stationary servers. More or less, yes. At least, the idea of networking. It is also the key to my concept of the SuperSmart Grid. Because we need both, Super Grids and Smart Grids, we combine them, take advantage of their synergies, and interweave the various approaches and networks! That is the only way to achieve 100 percent renewable energy.

Ulrich Dietz Like many innovative ideas, this one too sounds astonishingly obvious. But how utopian is it—still?

Antonella Battaglini The goal is to construct this network, a SuperSmart power grid.

Ulrich Dietz What is the SuperSmart element?

Antonella Battaglini It transports not only electricity but also information! That is why its network structure can be compared to the Internet.

Ulrich Dietz In what way?

Antonella Battaglini Imagine that tomorrow all kinds of energy would flow not just through the Internet but also through the power grid!

Ulrich Dietz The power grid?

Antonella Battaglini Yes.

Ulrich Dietz What do you mean by "tomorrow"?

Antonella Battaglini According to our studies, a SuperSmart Grid would be possible in Europe as early as 2050. That is an important date, because by then our power supply system will have to be carbon-free worldwide. We already have the technologies. All we need is to activate them with immediate help from the political and business worlds in the form of new regulations and directed investments.

Ulrich Dietz If your SuperSmart Grid philosophy prevails, then at some point every resident of our planet can chose his or her optimal mix of energy in a complementary way. A terrific utopia, but where are the limits?

Antonella Battaglini Above all, there are political hurdles to overcome and the associated investment risks have to be assessed, and they too are accompanied by political uncertainties.

Ulrich Dietz What difficulties do you face when explaining your SuperSmart Grid to energy companies?

Antonella Battaglini First, I am not an engineer and, second, I am a woman. And I operate in a man's world. At first they thought I was crazy: a woman without the relevant background! But in the meantime the SuperSmart Grid has been getting more and more response internationally. It is important that the public understands the different objections of the various lobbies, realizing, for example, that part of the industry is advocating a mix of 40 percent nuclear energy, 40 percent fossil fuels such as coal, oil, and gas, and 20 percent renewable electricity, whereas we consider it financially feasible to have electricity from 100 percent renewable sources.

Ulrich Dietz Can you present budgets that show that?

Antonella Battaglini We have to create attractive business models for investing in 100 percent renewable electricity. Capital is not the sticking point. In the decades to come, hundreds of billion euros and dollars will be invested in the energy economy. The SuperSmart Grid will scarcely be more expensive than traditional electricity production. Rather than investing in nuclear and coal power plants, we can advance renewable energies, a European market for electricity, solar power from the Sahara, electromobility, and so on…But to achieve that we have to be prepared to transcend the boundaries of parties, associations, companies, countries, and mentalities.

Ulrich Dietz Which is a worthy goal.

Antonella Battaglini Exactly. We have to have a pan-European and transterritorial approach. Use the capacity for hydroelectric power in Scandinavia, the sun in the desert of North Africa, the wind in Northwestern Europe, biomass in Eastern Europe, and so on. That is to say, energy sources wherever they can be exploited efficiently.

Ulrich Dietz You are alluding to the new industry initiative Desertec, which seeks to produce renewable electricity in North Africa and export it to Europe.

Antonella Battaglini Precisely. Ideally, we have to merge the SuperSmart Grid and Desertec in order to finance 100 percent renewable electricity. One of the major problems is the difficulty of balancing supply and demand worldwide.

Ulrich Dietz Can you give an example?

Antonella Battaglini Our electricity grid turns out to still have a number of holes, because everyone insists on his or her standpoint. For example, the price of electricity reached a peak on October 14, 2008, a Sunday. It was very windy, so a lot of electricity was being produced, but little of it was needed. It could neither be stored nor transported. If we had had a network to transport it over great distances with little loss and had had an integrated European electricity market, the electricity could have quickly been directed to places where it was needed.

Ulrich Dietz What is lacking?

Antonella Battaglini Transmission capacity.

Ulrich Dietz Another problem is that there are various electricity companies who own the different grids. That is why it is urgent that the production of electricity be separated from its sale.

Antonella Battaglini That is already happening through the unbundling process, in which the production of energy is separated from the associated grids. For example, Vattenfall is selling its grid, and TenneT, the Dutch grid administrator, has already purchased EON's.

Ulrich Dietz Electricity prices and grid tariffs should be optimized to minimize the possibility of price agreements between electricity providers and thus make competition more open.

Antonella Battaglini Yes, the EU Commission is pushing for such unbundling, which is extremely important to the supply of electricity across borders.

Ulrich Dietz What is your role in this process?

Antonella Battaglini In January 2009, Guido Axmann and I, with the support of the European Climate Foundation, founded the Renewables Grid Initiative, which is bringing together for the first time transmission system operators such as TenneT and 50Hertz (formerly Vattenfall), and nongovernmental organizations such as the WWF and Germanwatch.

Ulrich Dietz What do you want to achieve?

Antonella Battaglini For example, that electricity from local, decentralized sources of renewable energy can flow completely into the power grids, such as electricity from offshore wind parks and solar power plants. It also has to become easier to invest in electricity transmission lines and in both direct and alternating current technology. And innovative Smart Grid technology should be introduced to reduce costs. As I have said, the grid infrastructure has to be fundamentally renovated.

Ulrich Dietz Some time ago you launched TheCompensators*. What sort of compensation is it concerned with?

Antonella Battaglini TheCompensators* is a nonprofit association I founded with two colleagues, Armin Haas and Hannah Förster. We remove emissions allowances from the European emissions trade. The more the available emissions allowances can be reduced, the more the price for CO_2 emissions will rise. Anyone can get involved in climate policy in this way. After all, every German produces nine to twelve tons of carbon dioxide annually. Our goal is to be active globally, not just in Europe.

Ulrich Dietz Your chances are good. At least since the largely unsuccessful climate summit in Copenhagen in December 2009, many more politicians, entrepreneurs, and the public have come to understand how urgent it is to intensify and accelerate efforts to achieve this goal.

Antonella Battaglini That is true. In the meantime we have powerful allies from politics and business. Even Areva, the international market leader in the field of nuclear energy, is producing solutions for electricity production from renewable sources. Very many companies are now investing in renewable energy and integrating it into their systems. Gradually, everyone involved is learning what their specific technologies can contribute and how all of them can be connected.

Ulrich Dietz Building this infrastructure is a laborious process.

Antonella Battaglini Yes, it takes years. Like the good old game of Lego, you join one piece to the next. We have to combine all the available energy sources and initiatives. It is about the coexistence of every conceivable scale and distance on every level.

Ulrich Dietz So in the future even my electric car will be able to store electricity?

Antonella Battaglini Exactly. That is why we should no longer be speaking solely of distributing energy but also of effective distribution of storage. Electricity has to flow freely, like information.

Ulrich Dietz Does your Renewables Grid Initiative also work with the Desertec coalition?

Antonella Battaglini Yes. Desertec's goal for 2050 is to produce 15 percent of the electricity needed in Europe from renewable energy sources in North Africa—in addition to electricity from renewable energy that North Africa itself will use. We support this vision and are cooperating with Desertec to produce joint business models for investing in electrical grids that will be able to provide 100 percent renewable electricity forty years from now.

Ulrich Dietz And other partners?

Antonella Battaglini Recently we began working with PricewaterhouseCoopers, one of the largest consulting companies in the world, on a road map and case studies for politicians.

Ulrich Dietz There is an enormous amount of translation work you will have to do.

Antonella Battaglini That is true, but I love mediating between very different partners and finding the common denominator.

Ulrich Dietz Is it your innovative talent for putting together the pieces of the puzzle in complex systems?

Antonella Battaglini I believe my biggest talent is networking. I am quicker to see points of connection and come up with concepts for intelligent fusions and mergers. It is a game of patience, and hopefully it will pay off.

Ulrich Dietz The market for alternative energy sources is a multibillion dollar market. I am firmly convinced we can count on considerable momentum from it in the coming years, almost a kind of self-fulfilling prophecy.

Antonella Battaglini That would be my greatest reward. My message is always the same: 100 percent electricity from renewable resources is possible and affordable—if we all want it. It is our future.

Josh Bernstein

"Entrepreneurs are the explorers of the business world."

Josh Bernstein

He combines in an ideal way an urge to
explore and a thirst for adventure. Born in
New York in 1971, Josh Bernstein studied
anthropology, psychology, and Native
American and Near Eastern Studies at the
Cornell University in Ithaca, New York.
He was only seventeen when he began studying survival in extreme conditions at the
Boulder Outdoor Survival School (BOSS).
After completing his studies, he became a
trainer and teacher there and ultimately
president of the school. Shortly thereafter,
he was discovered by the History Channel,
where from 2005 to 2007 he had great success
by revealing to the public the most mysterious
ancient sites in the world. On the Discovery
Channel, to which he then switched, he
had record ratings. Currently he is working
on a series of children's books and a new
television production.

Hardly anyone knows the world better than he does, and few have explored it in such adventurous ways, diving, rock climbing, cycling, paragliding, and hiking. We meet Josh Bernstein in the enormous library of the classy Cornell Club on Forty-fourth Street in New York. He is sitting sunk into a heavy Chesterfield chair, leafing through a book. In his classic tweed jacket, he looks more like an English land-owner than the daring explorer and discoverer who became a media star through his shows for the History Channel and the Discovery Channel in the United States. Our conversation reveals that he is not a daredevil but rather a very contemplative, sensitive man. And he confirms the old truism: travel educates, both the mind and the heart.

Ulrich Dietz Some people see you as a real-life Indiana Jones. You are an archaeologist, scientist, adventurer, and survival expert. What was the crucial factor in your unusual biography?

Josh Bernstein When I was almost fifteen years old, my father died unexpectedly in his sleep of a heart attack. A year later, my twin brother, Andrew, and I lost our three-year-old sister in a car accident. Both of those experiences profoundly influenced my development and, looking back now, I would say they set me firmly on a path of self-reliance and independence. It may have been subconscious, but I was drawn to experiences that developed a person's confidence and control of the environment around him.

Ulrich Dietz Is that what drew you to nature and the wilderness, even though you grew up in New York?

Josh Bernstein That was certainly part of it. At first, I fell in love with the romantic imagery and mythology of the American West—from the gunfighters to the Native American cultures. In time, I grew to love the mountains, the deserts, and the people of the Four Corners area. Today, I love what New York City has to offer, too—the museums, the theaters, the restaurants. It was certainly challenging to maintain a foot in each world, but most of that was worked out while I was in college.

Ulrich Dietz The renowned Cornell University in Ithaca, New York…

Josh Bernstein …I loved my time at Cornell. I majored in anthropology and psychology, with a number of courses in Native American studies and Near Eastern Studies. After college, I spent a year in Jerusalem, studying Judaism and mysticism. It was then I decided I wanted to make a career for myself in the outdoor industry, so I returned to the United States and moved to Colorado.

Ulrich Dietz What kind of job did you have?

Josh Bernstein At first, I had a number of jobs. I had already been a guide at BOSS, the Boulder Outdoor Survival School, for a few summers and was hoping to make that into a year-round position. So I struck a deal with the owner of BOSS, creating a position as their marketing and administrative director. At the same time, though, I was doing photography, graphic design, and publishing on the side—just in case the survival school thing didn't work out. Thankfully, it did and I've stayed with BOSS since 1994, eventually becoming CEO and owner in 1997.

Ulrich Dietz What do you learn there?

Josh Bernstein The BOSS curriculae focus on primitive technologies—how people lived in harmony with the earth before the influence of modern technology and industry. Basically, we turn the clock back to a time when people made cutting edges from stones, cordage from plants, and clothing from hides. The goal is immersion in a world both completely foreign and yet oddly familiar in the primal sense. On one level, you're learning the skills you need to provide for yourself and others—how to make fire, how to trap food, how to navigate. On a deeper level, though, you're learning about yourself. Some of our courses are designed to be physically challenging; all of our courses are designed to give you greater confidence and a sense of self-reliance. We empower people.

Ulrich Dietz That sounds exciting. Who are your customers?

Josh Bernstein The majority of our clients are active, adventurous adults from the United States—people who are interested in challenging themselves, in learning something new, and in growing from the experience. Our average client last year was thirty-five years old, but the age ranges from eighteen to seventy-three. We care less about your age and more about your commitment to the course and what we can teach you.

Ulrich Dietz I hear you sometimes sleep in a yurt in Utah.

Josh Bernstein I do! I love my yurt. I've had a twenty-one foot yurt in Utah since 2001. Of course, my yurt meets building codes, so it's modern and has electricity, telephone, etc. My friends in Mongolia would be shocked to see my yurt, but the core architectural features—the lattice walls, canvas shell, compression ring and dome window—are the same. Now that I'm engaged, my fiancée and I are considering expanding the yurt and adding a bath house and guest room—we'll see.

Ulrich Dietz With your school you have found a niche and a smart business model: you sell expensive courses, for which your customers receive as little as possible!

Josh Bernstein Well, that's one perspective. The truth, though, is that the field experience at BOSS only appears to be Spartan. There's a whole back-end operation to the school that clients don't see. More importantly, though, I believe BOSS offers good value. After all, what price do you put on a person's growth? We take people somewhere, physically and metaphorically, where they likely couldn't go on their own.

 Perhaps I should take a course at your school, preferably with my employees. Survival training can never hurt in the business world. It would probably help me that I lived in the Black Forest, which used to have few comforts in its barren areas…

Josh Bernstein Then you'd certainly have some advantages! But I'm sure we could find some ways to push your buttons, too. And yes, our corporate training courses have been powerful experiences for the right teams. We also do courses for VIPs, celebrities, and media people. For example, BOSS did the consulting for the survival skills that appear in the island scenes of the movie *Cast Away* with Tom Hanks.

Ulrich Dietz You yourself became a star in 2005, with your series *Digging for the Truth* on the History Channel. What made it a hit?

Josh Bernstein Well, I think *Digging for the Truth* was the perfect combination of a number of factors. First of all, it was an ambitious effort from the History Channel to breathe new life into the documentary format. Instead of just talking about mysteries, they wanted the host to go to each location and meet the experts on site. Secondly, they decided to pick a host—me—who was younger than their typical host. And finally, they selected a production company (JWM Productions) that could package the adventures in a way that was both intellectually satisfying and aesthetically appealing. I think all three factors combined to give viewers something both entertaining and educational—a rare mix in television these days.

Ulrich Dietz Which experiences were high points for you?

Josh Bernstein The whole series! After all, I got to dive, climb, hike, bike, rappel, and paraglide my way around the world. And I got to see things few people ever get to see—hidden tombs, sacred chambers, secret rituals. There were so many fantastic experiences. If I had to pick three, though, I'd definitely say learning to shoot a traditional horn bow on horseback in Mongolia was a blast, as was visiting the highest relieving chamber in the Great Pyramid at Giza. And, finally, during the show I did on the Da Vinci Code, I was left completely alone in the Louvre with the Mona Lisa. It was surreal!

Ulrich Dietz As unforgettable as such expeditions were, above all they presumably meant hard work in both the conception and execution?

Josh Bernstein Absolutely. It was a brutal pace to create those shows. Each episode took two weeks to film, and we shot two or three episodes back-to-back. On some days, based on our location, I might film parts of three or four different shows. For me, it was non-stop travel for eight or nine months each year, with only a week off every month or two. At the time, I thought this was normal. Now, though, I know what a challenging production schedule that was and how lucky we were I managed to persevere.

Ulrich Dietz Since 2007, you have a new series, *Into the Unknown*, which you produce yourself for the Discovery Channel. How does it differ from the first show?

Josh Bernstein It is less about archaeological mysteries and more about mysteries in general. For example, we did a show about the possibility of life on Mars coming to Earth. I did another on elephants and the challenges they face in Africa right now. I loved doing an archaeological series, but at this point, I'd rather be an explorer of all things—past, present and future. Technology and privatized space travel, for instance, are interesting areas that I'd love to explore further. Who knows, perhaps I can take part in Richard Branson's Virgin Galactic operation.

Ulrich Dietz So would I.

Josh Bernstein In the meantime, though, I'm just completing a much-needed break from all the travel and, in the next few months, will be getting my newest series off the ground. I can't tell you much about it right now, but it will continue to be adventurous and international. I'm also working on a series of children's books that I hope will inspire the next generation to travel and explore.

Ulrich Dietz Do you consider yourself more a scientist or an adventurer?

Josh Bernstein Actually, I consider myself neither. If I had to pick a title, I'd go with explorer and educator. Adventurers are, in my opinion, people who are looking for an adrenaline rush. They seek the thrill of doing something new, something wild. Explorers, on the other hand, seek to gain some knowledge from an experience that benefits the world. It's often related to the sciences—a new species, a new territory, a new dimension—but it's not necessarily tied to pure scientific study. Exploration happens at the fringes of the known world; it's when people go beyond what's familiar and hope to find something unexpected or new. That's what interests me, and thanks to the medium of TV, I can often bring people along on my journeys. That's where the educational part comes in.

Ulrich Dietz It is the same way for me as an entrepreneur. There are lots of parallels between entrepreneurs and scientists. Both have to be in a position to cross boundaries and take risks. They are rewarded by discovering unknown regions of the globe or developing fascinating new products. Both are attracted by unfamiliar terrain, which they explore, which they want to dominate. That mobilizes creativity, strategic talent, and team spirit.

Josh Bernstein Exactly. Above all, the goal is to make the world better. Entrepreneurs are the explorers of the business world—people who can see beyond the maps of spreadsheets and business plans and want to venture into new territories. What's exciting now is that entrepreneurs are turning their attention to global challenges like stopping malaria, or creating clean drinking water, or preserving wildlife habitats. People are becoming more socially sensitive to the environmental impacts we have on the world and they're starting to act more responsibly with our nonrenewable resources. I'm both hopeful and encouraged.

Ulrich Dietz Exactly, and every one of us has to make a small contribution to that. What do you think: Is our higher social empathy a consequence of a need for the genuine, for authenticity? And is that why the reality TV you do is omnipresent everywhere, on European television too?

Josh Bernstein I'm a big fan of authenticity. So much of what we see on TV is manipulated and packaged in a way that attracts viewers but devalues humanity. It's made for the lower common denominator of our society—our ability to enjoy other people's suffering. I don't take pleasure in that. Television is an incredible medium for global connection. I'm grateful that the shows I've done are now seen in over 170 countries around the world. As much as I can, I want people to appreciate our cultural heritage, diversity and commonalities.

Ulrich Dietz You radiate the authenticity that so many people seek. Is there a point of intersection with innovation?

Josh Bernstein Absolutely! Technology today is making it easier and easier for people to connect globally. Facebook and Twitter, for example, connect hundreds of millions of people every day in a way that was incomprehensible just a decade ago. The result is

that our collective consciousness becomes more responsive, more dynamic, more aware. As more and more people see through false ideologies and start to connect with each other emotionally, barriers will come down and new dimensions will open. It becomes less about personal financial gain and more about sustainability and respect for everyone.

Ulrich Dietz Most founders and entrepreneurs know that too. They are not driven by the desire to make the big bucks but by an enthusiasm to develop something new.

Josh Bernstein Yes. And I'm hopeful that that "something new" will be a new paradigm for how our world operates.

Ulrich Dietz Are you a romantic?

Josh Bernstein Perhaps more of an idealist than a romantic. I'm too practically-minded to lose myself completely in romantic notions. And my years on the trail as a survival instructor have taught me how to be both realistic and opportunistic, when needed. Overall, though, my travels have taught me that the human experience is not unique to any one culture. At our core, there's a spectrum of emotions moving from fear to love. I prefer to operate closer to the "love" side and am hopeful others in the world want to do so, as well.

Ulrich Dietz Did you also address the theme of sustainability in your shows?

Josh Bernstein Not yet, although I hope to in the future. Right now, it's a tough proposition, as people aren't interested in watching television to have someone preach to them about sustainability. The message has to be carefully crafted in a way that is informative but not oppressive. Honestly, I recognize that our culture in the United States has to be weaned off of certain things. We are a consumer culture that is out of control and imbalanced. But the process takes time and a one-hour show is not the best approach at this moment. Independent documentaries and feature films are better, in my opinion, as they can be privately funded and the message won't have to be diluted or altered as much as television requires.

Ulrich Dietz Do you feel under pressure?

Josh Bernstein I feel the stakes are high and they're only going to get higher. Much of our media and governments are controlled or strongly influenced by institutions and multinational corporations that have invested a lot in the current system. Even if we know that the system is unfair or unsustainable, there's a lot of pressure to keep it in place. True, it will cost a lot to make the changes that are necessary, but it will cost a lot more if we do nothing and just continue along our current path. I feel pressure from that.

 It's unfortunately the reality. So far, only the campaign against smoking has been successful worldwide. Most of the other initiatives to improve the environment have been almost entirely without effect.

Josh Bernstein It's a shame, and so things will get worse before they hopefully get better. Global air pollution will increase; more species will die out; the rain forest will shrink further; and the polar caps will melt.

 Your survival techniques could become even more important.

Josh Bernstein Imminent catastrophes are not my motivation.

 Your approach is the right one. Even if the world is still moving in another direction, your work sets a course that has an effect. Could you, in conclusion, offer your three ultimate travel tips for a trip into the unknown?

Josh Bernstein Gladly. First: be open-minded and adventurous. Second: be humble and respectful of other people's cultures and their ways of doing things. And third: travel with a sense of humor! Life's too short to be in a bad mood.

Amar Bhidé

"The desire to consume has an innovative element."

Amar Bhidé

He is considered as one of the leading experts on innovations in business. Born in Delhi in 1949, Amar Bhidé moved to the United States as a child with his family. Until 1977, he studied at the Indian Institute of Technology in Delhi, then went to the Harvard Business School where he received his MBA in 1979. After nine years as a management consultant at McKinsey and the financial services company E. F. Hutton, he returned to Harvard in 1988 and began an academic career, which took him to Chicago, Columbia University in New York, and finally back to Harvard University in Cambridge near Boston. His most recent book, *A Call for Judgment: Sensible Finance for a Dynamic Economy,* is a passionate appeal to return as quickly as possible to a real economy of personal relationships.

Where does one meet a researcher if not where he works? But Amar Bhidé's office at Harvard is so tiny that we go looking for a quiet place for our interview in the halls of the building. We find it in a corner opposite a lecture hall, where an evening lecture is taking place. The noise level does not bother the Indian scholar in the least. His voice is that much quieter—a practiced trick to generate attention. Calmly he explains his theories, patiently answering questions. He seems to enjoy the sometimes controversial conversation. Bhidé has studied more closely than anyone how Americans and Europeans differ in their demand for consumer goods, and he advises the Old World to learn from the New World. Gradually the enormous lecture hall empties. The professor takes one of the seats in the auditorium to pose for the portrait, and suddenly he looks as young as one of his own students.

Ulrich Dietz The enthusiasm and ambition of Indian entrepreneurs, the likes of Ratan Tata or Sunil Mittal, excite me. Is there a secret to the success of Indian entrepreneurship?

Amar Bhidé The answer will surprise you. But first I wanted to ask you if you happen to know a friend of mine from university, Nandan Nilekani.

Ulrich Dietz No, should I?

Amar Bhidé Definitely, you're both in the same industry. Until the middle of 2009, Nandan Nilekani was CEO of Infosys Technologies, India's second-largest IT service provider, and now he is chairman of Unique Identification Authority of India, which is planning ultramodern identity cards.

Ulrich Dietz Of course I have heard of Infosys, and I know N. R. Narayana Murthy especially well, one of its founders and Chairman of the Board. I'd like to meet your friend the next time I'm in India.

Amar Bhidé Just let me know. Now to your question. It's very simple: Indian business people have adopted the American model with its focused thinking and action. They studied in the United States and imported it to their homeland.

Ulrich Dietz Can it be reduced to such a common denominator?

Amar Bhidé In my view, there is nothing truly new in a modern economy, but also nothing static. Economic competition in the twenty-first century is based largely on copying one another. I mean that in a positive way, since it increases profit if you adopt what has been successful and alter it slightly. It's human nature to repeat things with slight modifications.

Ulrich Dietz You mean that one varies and improves on it?

Amar Bhidé Exactly. The Book of Ecclesiastes in the Bible already said it: there is no new thing under the sun. This contrasts with Heraclitus' formulation: panta rhei, or "everything flows." You do not step into the same river twice. These two wise sayings, however contradictory, are equally true. For example, on the one hand, Infosys is a brand-new business idea, especially in relation to the measurability of services; on the other hand, it is based on American management theory. In most cases, an innovation is nothing more than an idea transferred to another context.

Ulrich Dietz Does that mean you consider it innovative when high-wage countries outsource production and development to low-wage countries?

Amar Bhidé Absolutely. I'll give you an example. Do you know where Henry Ford got the idea for the conveyor belt he used for the Model T?

Ulrich Dietz You mean the Tin Lizzie, of which more were sold than any car in the world until the VW Beetle beat its record in 1972. No, I don't, but I'm anxious to hear!

Amar Bhidé From the slaughterhouse. Originally at Ford each part was produced on site, by different people. The production of meat, by contrast, was organized such that the meat passed on a belt through the various stations of its production. Ford copied this process and thus revolutionized the auto industry.

Ulrich Dietz In a sense, the outsourcing and offshoring practiced in the United States more than any other country is the final stage of the assembly line. More and more tasks that until now have been done internally are outsourced to countries with lower wage costs and better conditions. In software development and production in particular, entire company processes are being outsourced today, from customer service in call centers to personnel management, payroll, accounting. Thus far China and India have been the favorite locations for such outsourcing, because labor is cheaper there. But isn't it also a threat to an economy? Isn't it more intelligent in the long term to improve logistics and organization at the production site and thus to keep costs down so that higher wages can be paid? For me at least, outsourcing is just one instrument of globalization among others. Sooner or later, companies will have to develop other profitable business models.

Amar Bhidé Right. Although I believe the negative consequences of outsourcing are greatly overemphasized.

Ulrich Dietz How so?

Amar Bhidé No one, whether in the United States or in other countries that use offshore services and outsourcing, has ever lost his or her job for that reason. The jobs do not disappear. Rather, thanks to increasingly refined technologies, equal numbers of new jobs are created in parallel. For example, more and more specialists are needed, in the information, knowledge, and culture sectors. New technologies produce new requirements that preserve the balance of supply and demand.

Ulrich Dietz Agreed. However, I consider the central thesis of your book *The Venturesome Economy* to be very risk-friendly. You claim that consumption encourages innovations. It reminds me of the thesis that Wolfgang Reitzle advocated: "Luxury creates prosperity." Reitzle is now Chairman of the Board of Linde AG, the international market leader in industrial gases. He wrote the book in 2003.

Amar Bhidé It seems that other people share my opinion. The desire to consume has an innovative element. It is an expression of a fundamentally optimistic, happy society. Send people shopping! Seriously, our increasingly advanced economies invent more and more products that need a market. If lots of people buy and consume them, they contribute to the society's potential to innovate. Think of Apple…

Ulrich Dietz …the computer company, which comes up repeatedly in other conversations in our book as well. The history of its success is unprecedented, and it culminated in Apple overtaking Microsoft in 2010 as the technology company with the highest market capitalization in the world, at 227 versus 223 billion dollars. In the middle of a world economic crisis!

Amar Bhidé Yes. Apple is innovative in being different. That is an essential element of innovation: every reformer has his own personal style. Steve Jobs shifted the focus of his company over the years from the technological to the commercial side. His idea to sell a single song rather than an album through iTunes was brilliant. Then there is the design. The unmistakable look Apple has created for its brand constitutes its innovation in the area of marketing.

Ulrich Dietz Apple is the unsurpassed number one in marketing in the global market. Do you think Americans in general are more innovative in their thinking, that is, more open to the new?

Amar Bhidé Do you mean in comparison to Europeans, especially the Germans? Well, in a survey I did one or two years ago, it seemed that way. I asked companies where they sell their products and services and what differences they observe in American or European customers. The finding was that US consumers were more willing to try new things, regardless of all bugs. German customers, by contrast, purchased new products only when they were sure they were almost 100 hundred percent functional.

Ulrich Dietz Germans are indeed inclined to be too careful. It's evident in all facets of life, even in politics!

Amar Bhidé A little less fear of the future would do them good. Do you know when Bank of America advertised in all the media that it would lend money to anyone buying a car?

Ulrich Dietz Perhaps 2005?

Amar Bhidé It was 1935, in the middle of the worst recession.

Ulrich Dietz Would a global campaign to consume more lead us out of the crisis?

Amar Bhidé I believe so. It would make consumers more willing to get excited about new products in all fields. Customers would invest more easily; they would be more likely to take risks. Every purchase of a commodity has an entrepreneurial component. You decide to acquire it. This active aspect of consumption has been criminally underestimated. Customers are now considered partners in companies. They comment on the goods they purchase, call attention to problems, and even propose solutions. Innovative offerings can therefore be tailor-made from the outset.

Ulrich Dietz I'm aware of these theses. Your colleague, the star economist Jagdish Bhagwati, has argued that Germany and China should spend more money, because it would help the entire world get out of the recession more quickly. But do consumer incentives really help? Haven't even the Americans recognized in the meantime that they cannot continue to accumulate debt? Or think of the smaller European countries such as Greece. They have lived beyond their means for decades.

Amar Bhidé Allow me to explain using the example of the United States: debt has been the reality in America for two centuries. It is part of the American lifestyle. People worry about today; everything else is bracketed out. So things keep moving, which is good. But at a certain point it becomes dangerous, admittedly.

Ulrich Dietz When households and companies can only finance loans with the hope of increase in value. And when companies finance others entirely through loans—that is, buy them and then burden the companies they have taken over with these debts, as many private equity companies did in recent years.

Amar Bhidé On the other hand, American companies spin off entire areas as soon as they become too large and unmanageable. American entrepreneurs have always been that way: they look unwaveringly forward and get down to work. The greatest strength of the United States is its ability to change. It should be a model for every other country.

Ulrich Dietz In accordance with the motto "the proof of the pudding is in the eating." Probably that attitude is not so far off in an economic crisis…

Amar Bhidé Yes, because it is inherently innovative. The positive thing about it is that the United States and Europe are coming closer together on this point. As recently as the nineteenth century, consumption was considered a sin in Europe. Only the aristocracy was permitted to live extravagantly and waste money; the common people lived on the edge of the subsistence level. That only changed with the beginning of mass production. Today the entire world imitates the consumption-fixated model of the USA, newly industrialized countries just as much as Europe. Even in Germany, fortunately, people no longer save as tenaciously. Instead, your compatriots travel, go to restaurants, and enjoy their wealth more than ever before.

Ulrich Dietz Do you mean that the world in general is becoming more hedonistic and pleasure-seeking? Because I come from a Protestant background, I have reservations about that.

Amar Bhidé I think so. But consumption is just one aspect. Just as decisive is the increasing individuality that goes along with it. It too promotes innovation.

Ulrich Dietz I consider it crucial to have an education that encourages students from the outset to ask why. It is the key to a progressive, responsible, and free society.

Amar Bhidé You said it. There was an article about it in the *New York Times* recently. A journalist questioned the generally accepted mathematical formula "a negative times a negative equals a positive," arguing that it doesn't make sense either that an enemy times an enemy equals a friend. This playful doubt regarding apparently valid truths has to be a crucial part of any education, much more important than rote learning.

Ulrich Dietz You must, however, also know the saying "The enemy of my enemy is my friend." Nevertheless, I believe that you get at the heart of innovation research with that. Calling things into question; surely every invention and every entrepreneurial idea begins with that. But otherwise, I find your example wonderful. When I add two debts, they rarely become positive. But to return to our theme: Isn't Chinese society a counterexample to our open, enlightened society? People are still educated to be yes-men.

Amar Bhidé That is also changing gradually. Rapidly increasing consumption will continue to make the Chinese more individual. No, China's biggest problem is pollution.

Ulrich Dietz That is indeed one of our greatest challenges. The problem can only be solved, however, if Western countries, and above all the United States, set an example by conserving energy. The way energy continues to be wasted in the country where you are living leaves me speechless. It doesn't help anyone to wait until the Chinese and the Indians finally become more environmentally aware.

Amar Bhidé It was a big mistake when oil prices fell in 2009. Apart from that, I believe that this problem will not be solved in the long run on an international level but on a national level. The United States, for example, will not worry about what China does, or permits but will raise the carbon tax enormously. Then solar energy can become more attractive; its cost will fall. After the disaster in the Gulf of Mexico, the explosion on the Deepwater Horizon oil rig and the resulting catastrophe, this trend will accelerate.

Ulrich Dietz Three years ago, I met Governor Arnold Schwarzenegger in Los Angeles. He really impressed me when he said that the movement will be where the investments are. At the moment investments in the Silicon Valley are increasingly moving into green energy and nanotechnology. But California is not America. Isn't it the case that countries such as China, Korea, India, and Brazil that are growing quickly pose an environmental threat to the rest of the world because they pollute the planet disproportionately?

Amar Bhidé That doesn't help at all. Here again we have to place our hopes in new technologies that are energy-efficient or based on recycling and so permit growth while still reducing the carbon dioxide concentration in the atmosphere.

Ulrich Dietz Will the newly industrialized countries — above all India—soon overtake Europe in terms of economic capacity?

Amar Bhidé Well, most European countries already reached their economic peak twenty-five years ago. In India, for example, we are still far from it. Currently half a billion people are moving from the country to the city. That is an incredible chance but also a source of incredible problems. This process will initially change the world completely, since it is happening with enormous speed. Something the Europeans had two centuries to do is happening in India in just a decade! People are moving into the cities because they earn more money and therefore they also spend more money on consumption. Real estate prices are increasing rapidly, but so are crime rates. The one accompanies the other.

 The price of progress. What hurdles does India still have to overcome?

Amar Bhidé The biggest one is its disastrous tax system. The government is practically broke; in February 2010 the national debt was 86 percent of its gross domestic product. The circumstances were comparable to the desolate situation in Greece during the same period. Above all else, India has to reduce social inequality. Because it leads to a large part of the population cheating on taxes or at least trying to do so.

 In light of the story of the Indian boom, do you want to return to your homeland soon?

Amar Bhidé No. I don't even spend my vacations there. I'd rather go to Europe.

 Why? That surprises me, since India is such a beautiful country.

Amar Bhidé Because I can pursue my career in peace here in the United States. India is too dynamic for me, too loud and dirty. I like clean air. Even with a lot of money I will not be able to buy that in Mumbai in the foreseeable future.

 I can tell you a story about that! Some time ago I bought a company in New York. The bosses arrived to sign the agreements, and we put them up in a hotel in the Black Forest. When we arrived the next morning, they said completely seriously: "We hardly slept; the air was far too clean and it was too quiet!"

Amar Bhidé A good story! The noise level some people need is a nightmare for me. That is why I was so happy to move from New York, where I first lived, to Boston. And New York is a quiet city in comparison with Mumbai.

 Over the past two years we have seen how the finance industry nearly ruined the real economy. In your view, should it be more regulated—also with an eye to keeping our society innovative?

Amar Bhidé I consider regulation nearly impossible. It is extremely difficult to regulate the banking industry. The first bank was opened in America in 1791. Until 1939 there were several crises and attempts to control them. Nevertheless, the country experienced constant economic progress. Like every crisis, a recession also requires change. In the economic sphere, it looks as though someone who a few years ago could still have bought a forty thousand dollar house can perhaps still afford a small car today. People just permit themselves different products. 90 percent of the people are still employed. If 30 percent of them lose their jobs in a stable economic situation, it is 35 percent in tough times. Even in the worst periods, overall consumption only falls about 3 percent.

 It is remarkable how much the balance of the world has already shifted to the East and the South. At the G 20, the forum for global financial questions, South Korea, the host country in 2010, clearly showed in June of this year how the newly industrialized countries will influence the world economy in the future. Do you welcome this development?

Amar Bhidé Absolutely. The newly industrialized countries will make a decisive contribution to ensure global prosperity. Nothing is more important than this change.

Murat Günak

"You need self-confidence to risk new ventures."

Murat Günak

He designed the dynamic body of the Mercedes SLR but Murat Günak has also come up with new looks for cars by Peugeot and Volkswagen. Yet this high-flier spoiled by success, who was born in Istanbul in 1957, had a crisis of faith in 2007. On short notice, he left Volkswagen, the enormous company in Wolfsburg, and with a partner cofounded Mindset AG near Lucerne, Switzerland. The goal: building electric cars that are not just ecologically correct but also look good. Günak has since developed two models: the aerodynamic sporty coupé Mindset and Mia, a small electric car for short distances that runs on lithium-phosphate batteries. By 2011, this cute, compact box on wheels will demonstrate that the philosophy of its inventors captures the zeitgeist: less is more.

At fifty, he dropped out. He left one of the biggest car companies in the world and began to develop his first electric car. Many considered the German-Turkish automobile designer and industry star to be crazy, but Günak believes more than ever in his vision of a pollution-free, silent electromobility. We meet him in the lobby of GFT Corporate Center in Stuttgart. He attentively regards the giant, walk-in fabric sculpture by the French sculptor Vincent Tavenne, a new acquisition. It has a theatrical quality, remarks the trained stage designer smiling. Over juice, coffee, water, and buttered pretzels in my office, he not only talks candidly about the pleasures and frustrations of his profession but also helps us to understand Turkish values. His farewell present: a children's book he wrote and illustrated himself.

Ulrich Dietz As the former star designer at Mercedes, Peugeot and, most recently, VW, you're somebody with a deep knowledge of the automotive industry. How capable of renewal do you consider these companies to be?

Murat Günak Without a doubt, their research departments are highly innovative when it comes to technology. On the other hand, scarcely any other industry is so secretive about its inventions. The experts monitor every detail, no matter how small, and the secrecy level is always maximum. The upshot is that the customer ultimately buys a product made in rather an authoritarian fashion. I don't imagine that will be possible in the future.

Ulrich Dietz And why not?

Murat Günak Today's consumers are ready for code-termination. Fewer and fewer people are prepared to buy often expensive goods without having any insight into the manufacturing process. Thanks to the Internet, people have been able to play a part in designing products for some time now. Everyone's an expert nowadays, up to a point. Anybody can produce a video and post it on YouTube, where it might be viewed by millions. Reviews posted by other readers sometimes persuade people to buy books from Amazon. This means our industry needs to learn to make better use of its customers' creativity.

Ulrich Dietz The arrogance of power appears to be pronounced among the major automobile manufacturers still. They only begin to think about new products when vehicle stockpiles climb to the five hundred thousand mark. Is sheer size an obstacle to a company's capacity for renewal?

Murat Günak Nobody in a big company dares to make mistakes.

Ulrich Dietz In 2001, we were supposed to create a new Internet portal for a big group. Fifteen people sat round the table during the discussions, everybody had plenty to say on the matter, but nobody was willing to take responsibility. Everybody delegated to others, and in the end the lowest common denominator was adopted as the standard.

Murat Günak That's because the engineers' expectations from standards are so high that the necessary investments are correspondingly enormous. And if two years later the product flops on the market, it's a disaster. If we don't manage to humanize these extreme standards soon, they'll bring down the entire industry in the end.

Ulrich Dietz I'm afraid it's not as simple as it sounds. Just imagine Rolex was to suddenly launch a digital wristwatch—wouldn't the customers be shocked more than anything else? That's why they make the hands a bit thicker, the logo a little bigger, and increase the price by a thousand euros. The customers pay for that. And apparently it's what the market wants. What prevented you from developing your electric cars at one of the companies you worked for?

Murat Günak At present, the manufacturers earn three percent per car, which is extremely low when you measure it against the expenditure. So the profit isn't generated by sales but by the vast industry that keeps a brand alive. It extends from the suppliers over the advertising people up to the workshops. Assuming all these sources of revenue were to vanish…

Ulrich Dietz It would be economically disastrous! That's why for years an entire industry has been putting up resistance to a quantum leap in electromobility. Most of the arguments disputing the economic feasibility of electric cars have meanwhile been refuted. It's only the massive pressure from Chinese industry, with its massive investments in electromobility and its determination to become a worldwide pioneer, that got the established manufacturers moving. How did you proceed with your products—the Mia electric car, for instance, or the Mindset sports coupé?

Murat Günak First of all we took a lot of care with product identification, which is very important in light of the rather negative public image of electric cars. Most of them look ugly, and don't inspire confidence in their everyday useability. And so we were aware of the need to design products that engage the senses. We hooked up with the tradition of automotive aesthetics, because we wanted to appeal to lovers of beautiful vehicles, with emphasis being placed on beautiful! Apart from that, our vehicles are supposed to supplement the other cars, not replace them.

Ulrich Dietz What do they look like?

Murat Günak Both cars are so-called commuters. The Mindset is more masculine in design. The first thing you notice is the huge, fully exposed twenty-two-inch wheels, and the circular headlamps. With an aerodynamic coupé body and box-like rear, the car is exactly 4.26 meters long, a four-seater with two continuous bench seats. And above all: it's wholly pollutant-free!

 It runs on a lithium-ion battery?

 Yes, in conjunction with a 70-kilowatt motor. Thanks to the aluminum frame and plastic body, the vehicle weighs a mere eight hundred kilograms. You can drive up to two hundred kilometers on the battery alone; we offer a 17-kilowatt range extender for distances up to eight hundred kilometers.

 What are the acceleration rates like?

 From zero to one hundred km/h in seven seconds. Top speed is 140 km/h, and there's a small solar-thermal plant on the roof of the Mindset. In good weather conditions that increases the action radius by another fifteen kilometers.

 What will the cars cost?

 The Mindset will sell at approximately fifty thousand euros, the Mia at under twenty thousand euros. The launch is foreseen for 2011 already.

 Which groups of buyers are you targeting?

 Customers who see themselves as trendsetters and want a cheerful vehicle that's fun to drive.

 So you've created the cult cars for the environment-friendly generation?

 We hope so. These vehicles translate into reality our philosophy of the lightness of being. That's how we see modern-day luxury: simple and fluid, uncomplicated and practical. Less is more! On the social plane, too, people are now more interested in cultivating networks than hierarchies.

 When did you begin designing the cars?

 Four and a half years ago, as soon as we were confident electromobility was set to make dynamic progress over the next ten years.

 A long time. What was so complicated?

 It was the rims in the case of the Mindset. The lateral acceleration of that vehicle is considerable, and there's a lack of empirical data on that subject. But the main problem with both cars is the financing. The resistance we come up against is enormous.

 Let's look down the road, after this bright beginning. You've designed promising new models. Now comes the difficult part: How do you gain market acceptance?

 It will be crucial that we are able to begin comprehensive sales and distribution the instant the cars are on the market.

 How will distribution function?

 Together with our German distribution partners we plan to deliver the vehicles first of all to firms maintaining vehicle pools, that is to say bulk buyers, and to municipal authorities. Those are customers for whom our product is very important. It signals emission-free mobility, cuts maintenance costs in the medium term, and reduces noise and pollution in town centres. Once the first step is in place, we'll be able to turn our attention to private customers, offering them direct service.

 One new trend is call service for repairs. Nespresso, the label of the Swiss Nestlé Group, is one example. They repair machines on site, or supply a replacement so that customers needn't go without their espresso even for a minute. I think it's an intelligent way of strengthening customer loyalty and promoting a brand. Why, actually, did you leave three companies in which you were very successful? Was it a matter of an overpowering vision, or a certain degree of frustration?

 I can't give you a short answer. I was lucky enough to join this industry in a phase when the need to extend the range of models was urgent. When I joined Mercedes in 1986, the company offered three models, no more and no less: the S-Class, the M-Class and the Baby Benz. Bruno Sacco, my boss at the time, gave me a lot of responsibility, although I was still quite young. I gradually acquired a reputation as a modernizer of car brands. That took me to Peugeot, who were almost bankrupt at the time. Paralyzed by fear, they balked at the risk of making a successor to the 205 and 206. That was my opportunity.

 You're bold. What other characteristics are needed to generate innovation specifically in the design field?

 Self-confidence. That answer might seem strange to you, but self-confidence comes from the gut! Forget market research and brand studies, that's all a load of pseudo claptrap. I always told my customers: I'll do it if you give me free rein. That's the risk you take, and I'll deal with the rest.

 After leaving Peugeot you returned to Mercedes, where you created the beautiful CLS coupé and the SLR super sports car.

 Fantastic vehicles, but despite that I ended up in a real identity crisis there. That's why I was happy when VW approached me in April 2003. Bernd Pischetsrieder, who was then CEO, shared my vision of turning VW back into Volkswagen, the maker of desirable, reliable cars at affordable prices. That was the story behind the Tiguan, the

new Scirocco, the Passat CC and the Golf 6. But unfortunately, unlike today, there was scarcely any interest in alternative forms of energy. At any rate, I reached a point where I thought: If I don't go now I never will.

Ulrich Dietz You and I, and a few other people I know, all roughly the same age, have achieved a lot in life. And now we all feel the same need: to initiate projects with substance. High-quality products and services that are technologically innovative, ecological and intended to benefit people.

Murat Günak We want to repay some of the opportunities to which we owe our careers. But that will only work if we avoid being elitist.

Ulrich Dietz Exactly. We both make high-quality products that are suitable for broad groups of buyers. Thousands of people use our banking solutions every day. And your cars ought to roll over the entire globe. Trailblazing innovations don't come about overnight, but over the next few years fundamental changes are going to shake up the market in our branch, too. I'm thinking of payment by mobile phone, for instance.

Murat Günak Information technology is set to considerably influence every area of our lives. The same goes for the automotive industry. Just think of the car2go mobility concept presented by Mercedes, its rental-car system for city centers. It's pure IT. And the sector still has to learn to utilize it more efficiently for new product offerings.

Ulrich Dietz Does your dual nationality make it easier for you to think "laterally," that is, to remain open to wholly new intellectual approaches?

Murat Günak I believe so. Let me tell you something about the Turkish upbringing. People often wonder why nations with a deep divide between rich and poor are so cheerful compared to other societies that, like Germany, possess an enduringly stable middle class. It's a question of upbringing. In Turkey, it's the person with the most experience of life who counts the most, not the one boasting the most titles or the most money. That's why respect for others plays such a big part, while here in Germany it's envy. In Turkey we learn as small children that a flower-seller might have a better life than a billionaire. That's liberating.

Ulrich Dietz Does it also make you more receptive to the new?

Murat Günak Yes, because we're capable of appreciating people as they are. In Germany, they prefer to keep people in check.

Ulrich Dietz Excessive control is poison for innovation, as we know. All the same, Germany sees itself as an innovative country.

Murat Günak And so it is, but mainly in engineering and technology, natural sciences and medicine, fields which tend to be dominated by intelligence rather than intuition. What are your roots?

Ulrich Dietz I'm from a family of entrepreneurs in the Baden-Württemberg region. My grandfather and my father worked in the jewelry industry.

Murat Günak What's your earliest childhood memory?

Ulrich Dietz The huge presses that were used to punch out the blanks in my father's jewelry factory. I was allowed to go to the firm with him from a very early age. The factory was a wonderful adventure playground. And I still remember having breakfast with the workers. Even today, the butter pretzel is the most luxurious breakfast I can have. When I was living in France and the United States, those regional specialties were the things I always missed most. It was my home region of Baden-Württemberg and the judicious technology policies of its government in the 1980s that allowed me to build up my company. I'm grateful for that. I'd like to mention the key word of respect. Respect for each other is elementary—also in regard to employees. I notice it over and over again: If I trust them, the best results come about. Free space seems to make people more creative.

Murat Günak Do you sometimes reward your teams?

Ulrich Dietz I believe that frank words and shared time are the best reward for all of us. I like spending a lot of time with the staff I work most closely with, and it gives people a chance to get to know each other. That's also the advantage of a family business like ours. The Board is within easy reach and it also thinks about the needs of the company's employees. What I want to say is: nowadays firms have to create conditions under which employees can identify with the company and its values and products. And in doing so they bring about economic growth.

Murat Günak I agree with you. One more remark about our products: if possible, they ought to liberate us too, not weigh us down. That's particularly true of the automobile, which was originally built to give people more freedom. It allowed them to discover the world, crucially contributed to the growing affluence of the Western hemisphere. In the post-war era, people celebrated the automobile for exactly those reasons. For instance, they decorated their cars with Gotthard stickers because they were so proud of having finally crossed over that mountain pass. I'd like to make my purchasers the gift of regaining that lightness of attitude towards the automobile as a product.

Ulrich Dietz Back to the roots in this case too?

Murat Günak Absolutely. A scratch on my cars shouldn't be a disaster, people should feel like writing the names of their sweethearts on the windowshield. Vehicles shouldn't be awe-inspiring fetishes but useful favorite toys.

Ulrich Dietz The cult people follow around this product is indeed singular, and considerably influences social behavior. Somebody who drives a BMW or Bentley or Ferrari dresses differently from somebody sitting in a Toyota, and behaves differently, too. I increasingly find myself wondering if it's even desirable to drive prestige cars today. In times when social conflicts are on the increase, it's not such a good idea to be conspicuous. Doesn't this make the role of the designer increasingly important?

Murat Günak Correct. Other industries can learn a lot from a model like the iPhone by Apple. It's an outstanding example of how sampling technologies can be used to speedily put a product on the market and then, thanks to the inspired design, build a consumer community that buys it millions of times over.

Ulrich Dietz In one of our business segments we procure and place freelance engineer and computer scientists. We manage around 1,500 specialists. Say a bank needs a team in Singapore, then we tailor a team, from technician to bank consultant, within a few days. Our experience suggests that more and more experts want to be self-employed in the future. It might be the case that for your electric vehicle you need a few engineers based in Japan. Or you need an engine made in Germany. And so on. If you're in a position to orchestrate the various specialists but have a strong brand at the same time, you can launch and position new products faster and, above all, more economically.

Murat Günak That's exactly the way I see it. It's about networking competence. We put together our small team of ten according to the same principle.

Ulrich Dietz But somebody has to organize this network, see to the maintenance and updating.

Murat Günak Maybe it would be possible to set up an Internet portal for that purpose, one that works like a market for applications. People would be accepted according to specific selection criteria and entrance tests, and contact would be taken up as required. Temporary employment agencies were the forerunners of this model, but they were more involved with basic services.

Ulrich Dietz We've advised various organizers of trade fairs this year. These events attract thousands of exhibitors and hundreds of thousands of visitors. The challenge is to link up the two sides in such a way that leads to synergistic effects and optimized encounters for everyone involved. After all, a fair brings together a community of individuals whose interest can be roused for related business fields, even ones that initially seem extraneous!

Murat Günak Absolutely, just think of the medium Internet. What I find so brilliant about it is that it supplies the user with unrestricted free space. True, it's fraught with risks, but it's fascinating how it is delegating the initiative completely.

Ulrich Dietz The consumer as producer?

Murat Günak Exactly. By the way, one classical business organization almost regained top place in its segment with the same strategy: Harley Davidson.

Ulrich Dietz Oh yes?

Murat Günak When you buy a Harley, it's the basic model, so to speak, with no accessories. But you get a thick catalog as well, and you can go through it and choose all the extras you want to create your own, unique machine! In that way, Harley Davidson triggers stories about the brand, making it increasingly popular and reclaiming the cult status it used to enjoy.

Ulrich Dietz The Germans are viewed as born inventors. What's the situation in Turkey?

Murat Günak In order to invent something, you need space to improvise. I wouldn't say Germany tops the league in that respect. On the other hand, it's one of the safest countries in the world, which makes living here especially pleasant.

Ulrich Dietz Chaos demands and promotes improvisation. I'm in Brazil a lot at present, especially in São Paulo. What I see there shows me that chaotic conditions can be creative, but also strenuous in the long run.

Murat Günak Especially if you're not used to chaos. I must admit I need a chaotic atmosphere to do the things I do as a designer. If the structures become rigid, it's time for me to go.

Ulrich Dietz At our company we strive to remain as flexible as possible. There are twenty-two offices, all of them geared towards multifunctional usage. My vision is to gather together on one site engineers and designers, academics and creative professionals from very diverse fields—small businesses but big firms, too. It could be the start of a kind of multi-creative think-tank with all kinds of exciting new linkage patterns.

Murat Günak I believe the future depends on this mixing of intellectual worlds and mentalities. Intelligent networking is set to be the magic formula of the twenty-first century, if you ask me.

"If you want to
be innovative,
you have to be
willing to fail."

DEEPFLIGHT
SUPER FALCON
SUPER FALCON
SUPER FALCON
COCKPIT EQUALIZE
DEEPFLIGHT

Graham Hawkes

The oceans have always fascinated him. But the trained engineer, born in London in 1947, first worked for the United Kingdom Atomic Energy Authority. There he discovered underwater defense technology and soon left for Plessey, where he was active in the underwater weapons unit in the 1970s. Then Hawkes went freelance and produced diving suits of fiberglass-reinforced plastic. This was followed by the founding of small, highly specialized companies, until he founded Hawkes Ocean Technologies (HOT) in 1996. With a four-person team, this pioneer has been developing spectacular underwater vehicles that glide through the water without harming the biosphere. His most famous customers include entrepreneurs such as Tom Perkins and Richard Branson.

It is a cool, windy day in Point Richmond, a district of Richmond, California, on the San Francisco Bay. Graham Hawkes's workshop is located at the yacht harbor; when you enter it, you think you are walking into a miniature airplane hangar. His wife, Karen, greets us, as Hawkes is on the phone. Standing in the middle of the room is the engineer's great pride: his Deep Flight Super Falcon, a kind of high-tech flounder in which you can fly underwater. For now, it is only being purchased by rich private customers for sporting pleasures, but soon industry and politicians will be interested in this racy vehicle. Hawkes has devoted every fiber of his being to his life vision, abandoning a well-paid position as an entrepreneur in London late in life, but he regrets nothing. Only now does he feel truly happy and free. It does not even bother him that the restaurant above the workshop, where the crew eats lunch almost daily, has only four choices on the menu: hot dogs, bacon and eggs, pizza, and spaghetti bolognese.

 For me, you are the Jules Verne of the twenty-first century. With your company Hawkes Ocean Technologies (HOT), you build spectacular winged submersibles for exploring the deep sea. When I heard of your Deep Flight, I was electrified. A genuine innovation in marine technology. How did you develop these underwater planes?

Graham Hawkes Like all new products, there is a long history behind them. In this case, it began with me, an engineer in marine technology, just wanting to build the next generation of cost-effective underwater vehicles. At the time, I had been rather successful designing manned and unmanned vehicles for scientific research, and for the military and civilian industry. But as my clients began to stipulate more and more the details of what I should do, I decided to take a radical step: I got out. I realized then that it was more important to me to realize my dreams than to get rich. So I sold some things, including my beloved sailboat, and founded HOT in 1996.

Ulrich Dietz Did you lose all your existing customers?

Graham Hawkes All of them. But that was the only way I could spend the next ten years concentrating on developing my prototypes.

Ulrich Dietz What was your core idea?

Graham Hawkes We wanted to develop a generation of lightweight, cost-effective vehicles to open the oceans for exploration. The key was to get the weight down so that our submersibles were not tied to expensive motherships. I was also looking to access all the dimensions of ocean space. Traditional submarines have a ballast system that enables them to dive; they are nothing more than a kind of vertical elevator, and hence they have limited horizontal maneuverability. With the Deep Flight submersible, by contrast, you are actually flying! They glide gracefully through water like dolphins, and like whales they can even do loops! Additionally, taking advantage of developments in lithium-ion battery technology and composites materials, our Deep Flight submersibles can travel to great depths and distances. We have also worked very hard to minimize the light and noise emissions from our vehicles, making them "green machines," and in our experience the animals do not flee from us but instead approach, and you can observe them and even play with them.

Ulrich Dietz Was it your ambition to travel and explore the oceans in a more environmentally friendly way, and your motivation to turn to undersea technology?

Graham Hawkes To be honest, at first I had no idea where my career would end up. After studying engineering, I worked for the United Kingdom's Atomic Energy Authority. I stumbled upon undersea defense technology by chance. In the 1970s, I was working for the Underwater Weapons Unit of the Plessey electronics company before I founded my first company with a partner. We designed and produced atmospheric diving systems, including the WASP and MANTIS diving suits of fiberglass-reinforced plastics. Then I founded and managed other small, highly specialized companies that produced, among other things, Remote Operated Vehicles (ROV) and, since the early 1990s, the Deep Flight manned vehicles themselves. So underwater technology became my main field—and it remains my great passion today. Because I discovered how far it lagged behind the times. It lacked money but above all it lacked imagination.

Ulrich Dietz And then you came along with little more than your imagination…

Graham Hawkes Something like that. In any case, that led to my little HOT laboratory, with just three or four colleagues, above all my wife, Karen. She is still responsible for organization, logistics, and finding sponsors. The great thing about our tiny company was that there was no time pressure, and we were no longer subject to the specifications of customers. At the time, reporters and managers kept asking me what goal I was pursuing with my models. My greatest satisfaction was replying: "None, none at all."

Ulrich Dietz Do you need that space in order to be innovative?

Graham Hawkes Absolutely. The feeling of freedom I have now is literally priceless! I have come to understand that you can only be innovative with a small team. As soon as a company has more than twenty employees, a critical point is reached. If you want to be innovative, you have to be willing to fail. You have to be hungry and cannot have anything to lose.

Ulrich Dietz That's why it's ideal to found your first company right after graduating or even while still in school. Because then you have more modest financial ambitions.

Graham Hawkes Yeah. When a company is fixated on becoming more and more profitable, and has a responsibility to several hundred employees, it can no longer be inventive. Understandably, since it has to concentrate on its customers and its products. If I were a large company, then I would have a division focused exclusively on start-ups and looking for talent in the industry to form project-based or longer term partnerships with them.

Ulrich Dietz I agree entirely! We too often work with small, independent companies with whom we contract on a case-by-case basis and then integrate more closely with our core team as necessary. Sometimes we are also financially involved in these companies, but then we emphasize that they need to retain their creative independence.

Graham Hawkes Do you see that as a trend?

Ulrich Dietz More like a necessary change in the labor market, which worldwide has to be more flexible, more mobile, and hence more creative. That works better with many small but well-networked teams of experts. You seem to have recognized early on the signs of the times. You are already in the fifth generation of development for your Deep Flights. What was your greatest challenge?

Graham Hawkes I always wanted to find a more elegant and above all more environmentally friendly way to move through water. As early as the 1980s I was experimenting with Deep Rover, a comparatively massive underwater vehicle that the director James Cameron used for his 3-D film *Aliens of the Deep*.

Ulrich Dietz With its stubby wings on the left and right and its acrylic dome, your Deep Flight submarine reminds me of an airplane.

Graham Hawkes You're right about that. It is also as maneuverable as an airplane. The wings also fulfill the same function, but with the difference that their shape works in the opposite direction. Whereas in an airplane they provide lift, a Deep Flight's wings create a more powerful downward pull that works against lift. The steering mechanism is also like that of an airplane. It doesn't sink like a stone but instead moves at an inclination of sixty degrees. You can fly curves with small radiuses just as quickly upward as downward.

Ulrich Dietz That's sensational. How quickly can you move with such a craft under water?

Graham Hawkes In the Deep Flight Super Falcon, two people can move underwater at speeds up to six knots, nearly 12 km/h. In Deep Flight I, we can fly about twelve knots, roughly 20 km/h.

Ulrich Dietz With you I feel a little bit like I'm in Q's workshop, the brilliant inventor of all the sophisticated toys in the James Bond movies.

Graham Hawkes You aren't so far off. The James Bond director John Glen used one of my older vehicles in his film *For Your Eyes Only*.

Ulrich Dietz In German it's called *In tödlicher Mission,* "On a deadly mission." Didn't Roger Moore play 007?

Graham Hawkes Yes. But the Wet Flight vehicle of 1998, which I constructed as a mobile camera platform from the outset, was a clear improvement over the MANTIS used at that time. In it we accompanied dolphins dancing in the sea for one movie. Imagine: we built it in just four months!

Ulrich Dietz You surely employ the most modern IT systems to plan your projects.

Graham Hawkes Naturally we employ 3-D CAD/CAM systems for construction, simulation, and calculation. But everything is done on standard Hewlett Packard work stations. All of the technologies we use are accessible to everyone.

Ulrich Dietz What software did you use for Deep Flight I, the prototype for all underwater planes?

Graham Hawkes We used Autodesk Inventor for that, because we could use it to simulate three-dimensional prototypes digitally, and no longer had to laboriously draw them and build models. In the old days, we would have needed thirty engineers, but now we do it with just four!

Ulrich Dietz What's the biggest advantage of the Inventor software for you?

Graham Hawkes I'll say it again more precisely: its adaptive functionality. For example, the software saves us countless calculations. We aren't overwhelmed by symbols and menus; the user interface is transparent and can be used intuitively. So we can continue to use existing data, and easily adapt elements from previous models to new ones. Moreover, I can study the flow of water and try out sequences of movements.

Ulrich Dietz So you can focus entirely on your creativity. That's a luxury. For me you are not just an engineer but also a pioneer. There are not a lot of them.

Graham Hawkes No, I'm a realist. People still don't understand the nature of this planet. In the United States alone there are five billionaires who have founded companies for spaceships and claim our future is on the moon or on Mars. But there's nothing up there but a good view. Our real future, our chances for survival, lie beneath us on the sea floor! 90 percent of life on earth is aquatic. It's hard to believe, but approximately only 5 percent of the world's seas have been explored! Yet the landscapes beneath the water's

EAN TECHNOLO

surface are just as diverse and exciting as those above. There are mountains, canyons, trenches, volcanoes, except no one has seen them because they are so deep.

 Is it true that you hold the world record for the deepest solo dive?

Graham Hawkes As far as I know, yes. When I tested Deep Rover, I went down to three thousand feet.

Ulrich Dietz Respect, that's about 915 meters below the surface. Who buys your deep-sea planes? Scientists or industry?

Graham Hawkes Not yet. So far, our customers have been more likely adventurers like the aviation pioneer and regatta sailor Steve Fossett. I built the deep-sea submarine Deep Flight Challenger for him. It can go down to 37,000 feet, nearly 11,300 meters, below the surface, and that is as far down as we have seen the ocean.

Ulrich Dietz You mean the Marianas Trench in the Western Pacific Ocean?

Graham Hawkes Exactly. You know that Fossett held records for, among other things, being the first to circumnavigate the earth in a balloon. Unfortunately he died in 2007 when his sport aircraft crashed in the Sierra Nevada Mountains.

Ulrich Dietz Isn't the businessman and venture capitalist Tom Perkins from the Silicon Valley one of your fans as well?

Graham Hawkes He bought a Super Falcon for 1.7 million dollars for his yacht *The Maltese Falcon*. At the time it was the largest private yacht in the world.

Ulrich Dietz So very interesting people come to your workshop in the San Francisco Bay Area. Could I actually drive the Falcon myself?

Graham Hawkes Absolutely. It's simple to operate. With its body of ceramic and epoxy resin, it is extremely light and especially stable under pressure. With its lithium-ion batteries, it can make many dives per day, and then still complete some night dives. You zoom down with propeller turbines, controlling it with a joy stick. The ailerons and control surfaces enable you to change in any direction. As with an Airbus, the horizontal and vertical stabilizers are controlled electronically.

Ulrich Dietz So someone can train to be a sea pilot in your flight school?

Graham Hawkes Yes. The course costs fifteen thousand dollars, but you will experience excursions you will never forget. For example, you will encounter giant manta rays or fly through a school of sharks. More than twenty pilots already have our license.

Ulrich Dietz And one of them, Richard Branson, has just purchased your Deep Flight Merlin, your most recent winged submarine, for his yacht *Necker Belle* and christened his exclusive, custom-built model the *Necker Nymph*.

Graham Hawkes And now he's enjoying it on his Necker Island in the Caribbean. We were there in the spring—it was paradise!

Ulrich Dietz Doesn't Branson market his own luxury catamaran as well?

Graham Hawkes Yes, when he's not using it himself with his family and friends. The *Necker Nymph* can be chartered for seven days for twenty-five thousand dollars. It has room for three people, the pilot and two others, who sit next to one another in an open cockpit. It can dive down to forty meters, and you enjoy a breathtaking panoramic view of the flora and fauna down there—a unique experience. Branson is obsessed, as am I.

Ulrich Dietz As our conversation—like the others in this book—demonstrates, innovation is always rooted in a deep passion for one thing.

Graham Hawkes That's right. I have become addicted to innovation. Commercial success is important to me only to the extent that it helps me continue doing what matters most to me.

Ulrich Dietz Even though it is the hardest way to make money?

Graham Hawkes You know the proverb "Necessity is the mother of invention?" It seems to prove true again and again.

Ulrich Dietz Yes. Crises and problems make people more creative. In German we say "Not lehrt beten" – "Adversity teaches you to pray." But no one can live in a permanent state of emergency.

Graham Hawkes More like in the yellow submarine of the Beatles. Surely it won't surprise you to hear that "Yellow Submarine" is one of my favorite songs.

Ulrich Dietz I like that song too: "We all live in a yellow submarine, yellow submarine…."

Edwin Kohl

"You need willful obstinacy to turn visions into reality."

Edwin Kohl

Crossover artist, an entrepreneur through and through—if these words apply to anyone, they apply to Edwin Kohl. Born in Merzig in 1949, he studied economics and worked as a product manager, but because he got bored, the honorary professor began to implement a profitable idea in 1979. He wanted to import pharmaceuticals from other countries with lower prices and offer them more cheaply in Germany. Within a few years, kohlpharma, a niche operation in Germany, had grown into the largest importer of medicines. In the years that followed, this resourceful strategist expanded the main brand to include three more, equally successful sectors. Not satisfied with that, Kohl has become involved in the green economy and has recently begun investing in Mia, a short-range electric car developed by Murat Günak.

He had the right idea at the right time, long before everyone else. And so Edwin Kohl of the Saarland became the largest importer of inexpensive medicines. He welcomes us at the entrance to his company in Merzig and leads us to his office, where paintings by local artists hang, as they do in the corridors and in the offices of his employees. The company building is a model of ecological, low-energy construction, which was an absolute must for Kohl. After our conversation, he offers us a tour through the buildings, normally kept secret, where his latest corporate baby, 7×4 Pharma, does its testing. We enter the rooms wearing protective clothing, and they turn out to be a first-class high-tech laboratory. This much robot chic cries out for an alternative world, and the hedonist Kohl takes us there for the final photograph: a magnificent country property with a spacious park and majestic trees, including his favorite old acacia.

Edwin Kohl May I begin by showing you a little film that tells you about what we do? It's an in-house production, and I'm especially proud to say all the actors are company employees! We invited them to casting sessions along with their families, and the whole project was a great success. Not least importantly, it boosted staff identification with the company and was entertaining as well.

Ulrich Dietz As an entrepreneur who runs his company like a large family business, are you faster, more emotional, than managers who have to consider investors' interests?

Edwin Kohl Definitely. I'll outline the corporate structure so that it's easier to understand. For thirty years, my main brand kohlpharma has been importing medicinal products purchased from pharmaceutical wholesalers around Europe. Alongside kohlpharma there's assist, a company I founded in 1992 to offer mobile care to invalids, who are visited at home by the some three hundred nurses we employ. The next business model, AVIE, emerged in 2004, a system partner concept for independently run pharmacies, which profit from the services rendered by AVIE. Finally, in 2007 I founded my youngest baby, 7×4 Pharma, which offers a highly complex, industrialized service. Its core is the 7×4 Box, which is a specially designed pack that contains, for each day of the week, automatically pre-sorted drugs for four different times of administration. It took almost eight years to develop the 7×4 Box and its production technology, at costs over one hundred million euros. That was the gamble we took and—here's my answer to your question—risks like that can only be sustained by a family business using its own money. We could never have done it if the company had been listed, or needed to seek the consent of investors in turn dependent on their own financial backers.

Ulrich Dietz We've been listed on the German Stock Exchange in Frankfurt for ten years now. But for me, there's nothing negative about having nonfamily shareholders; that's just as helpful as a constructively critical supervisory board. Over and over again, the Board forces me to substantiate my ideas, to think them through and present strong arguments. Thanks to a solid equity capitalization enabled only by going public, we can keep going down new paths in our own way—despite, or precisely because of, all the misgivings and opposition. So both models have their advantages and disadvantages.

Edwin Kohl Absolutely. Everyone has to choose the route that suits him or her best.

Ulrich Dietz When I look at your life's work, I'm bold enough to call you the Andy Warhol of the pharmaceuticals industry, because since 1979 you've regularly roused the opposition of the entire branch. In addition, I might add, your success matches that of the said artist.

Edwin Kohl Thank you! You're right, I'm somebody who enjoys breaking rules. Characters like that are often innovators.

Ulrich Dietz Because they have no choice. Is there a kind of genetic predisposition?

Edwin Kohl I believe so. After three years as a salaried product manager, I finally realized that I was somebody who enjoys going against the grain and is determined to implement his ideas without delay. I began by renting a disused one-room school for three hundred deutschmarks a month, installed an oil-fired stove, and started from scratch. I was determined to turn my idea into a big, long term business. I reckon you need that kind of wilful obstinacy in order to turn visions into reality.

Ulrich Dietz So you've been consistently overcoming medical-pharmaceutical barriers since embarking on your career?

Edwin Kohl Exactly. Every area of my company embodies a new model. And all of them roused the concerted opposition of hospitals, health insurers, or professional associations.

Ulrich Dietz Are you an idealist who wants to improve the world?

Edwin Kohl I'm a realist with a mission. That maybe explains why I'm quicker than the others to spot and analyse trends, for instance the demographic development. At present, two wage earners maintain one senior citizen, tomorrow one wage earner will have to provide the same level of support.

Ulrich Dietz That particularly applies to Europe. In the BRIC countries, that is to say Brazil, Russia, India and China, the situation is quite different.

Edwin Kohl That's true, but here in central Europe it means, for one thing, that we won't be able to afford the numbers of nursing homes and hospitals required in the future. When it comes to caring for the elderly we'll have to go down new paths such as those we explored with assist. Developing the project cost me several million euros, but now the annual earnings amount to several million likewise.

AVIE, for example, is based on a principle similar to that of the Edeka network of independent food retailers who buy as a group. We place a family brand in the hands of independent pharmacists in Germany. We've enlisted one hundred so far, and thousand is the target figure. It would be a mistake to become dependent on internationally operating pharmacy chains. We need to create our own distribution channels in order to ultimately project our jobs.

Edwin Kohl Yes. Namely that a society can only afford to care for an elderly population who remain living in their own homes for as long as possible. This premise is backed up by studies indicating that more than a million people were placed in homes and hospitals without this step being necessary. A major problem is the false or irregular taking of medication. The longer people live, the more medication they generally have to take. Frequently over ten different drugs per day. A therapy is only effective when the right medication is taken at the right dosage and the right time. My patented 7×4 Pharma system addresses this need.

Ulrich Dietz And what brought you into conflict with the health insurers, pharmacies and authorities in the process?

Edwin Kohl Some public authorities and health insurers don't think in an innovative way. Their inertia is sometimes very great. In fact they ought to invest much more in their clients' well-being, in order to be able to spend less on treatments. Some pharmacists still think I wanted to take their custom away. But the pharmacy is the central link in the chain of medication management. We've restricted our palette to four hundred medications, however.

Ulrich Dietz Making the logistics easier to handle?

Edwin Kohl Certainly, but the World Health Organization suggests that one hundred active substances would basically be sufficient. We offer four hundred because we concentrate on the most widespread ailments. But the pharma industry continues to loudly accuse us of compiling the thing it fears most: a so-called positive list of reimbursable medicines!

Ulrich Dietz You remain utterly convinced of your concept despite all these obstacles. I do too, by the way. Without breaking up this fateful alliance of pharma industry, health insurers structured like local authorities, the self-service mentality of patients, and the politicians with their thirst for quick results, there will be no possibility of reducing the costs of the health service.

Edwin Kohl You're right. It's a multi billion market!

Ulrich Dietz Let's talk about the details of this 7×4 concept.

Edwin Kohl The patient needs a pharmacy that collects and checks all his or her prescriptions. Using a special software the pharmacy sends us a data set every week with the current medication status, and from this data we produce the individual 7×4 box. It's series production, then, with a batch size of one—each of these weekly packs is different, but we can produce one hundred thousand of them a week. Anybody who becomes acquainted with this system will want to stick with the system, I'm convinced of that.

Ulrich Dietz Surely the nightmare of every process engineer: a combination of haute couture and prêt à porter, so to speak, of hand-crafting and mass production. All the same, I reckon your concept shows the way forward because there are no gaps in the information chain, all the way up to on-demand production.

Edwin Kohl It's highly complicated, especially the monitoring. During the manufacturing process each box is photographed tenfold and documented accordingly, so that it subsequently meets the requirements of the United States supervisory authorities.

Ulrich Dietz What are the greatest hurdles?

Edwin Kohl Convincing the health insurers to pay the weekly sum of four euros for this innovation, fifty-two weeks a year. We need approximately two hundred euros per patient. A small sum compared with the 1,300 to 1,500 euros a single referral to hospital would cost on the first day. We also assume that the box would considerably delay the point in time in which people move into nursing homes, again reducing costs incurred by the health system. But the negotiations are laborious; it takes a very long time to conclude a contract with a public health insurer.

Ulrich Dietz The biggest challenge you face, it seems to me, is persuading the various players with their own very special interests to gather round one table.

Edwin Kohl At least we have support from the political sphere, namely from the health minister, Philipp Rösler, and the chancellor, Angela Merkel.

Ulrich Dietz Hats off! You increasingly cover the chain of services from nursing over medication up to the pharmacies. The next step would be your own hospital.

Edwin Kohl No. The next step is internationalization. We're already having discussions with the responsible people in other countries. We've created something unique in global terms.

 Pulling off an invention of that kind is one thing, turning it into a lucrative business is another. What progress have you made?

Edwin Kohl We still need staying power. The profits made with kohlpharma and assist are ploughed back into AVIE and 7×4 Pharma. I'm privileged to own two cash cows as well as two cash-hungry calves.

Edwin Kohl No. We're problem solvers. That spurs us on every day. We'll file more patent applications when we've solved issues like how to make it clear exactly when a pill needs to be taken. Some are taken before meals, for instance, others after meals, but how do you communicate this to a patient who is practically blind?

Edwin Kohl Strictly pragmatically. But in this case it's too early to talk about it in public.

Edwin Kohl I'm no longer as involved in day-to-day operations. I'm responsible for making sure our companies will still be making solid profits in ten years' time. Ideas in that respect occur to me everywhere—when I'm exercising, sometimes even on the golf course. It might sound like a cliché, but it's where I relax, and that's what it counts.

Edwin Kohl You're right, one needs distance. Alongside health care for the elderly, by the way, my second major theme for the past twenty years has been ecological building management. My company headquarter in Merzig is a low-power building with minimal use of chemical pollutants.

Edwin Kohl That way the future lies! For our overhead heating or cooling we use geothermics in winter or the waste heat from the industrial plant in our neighborhood. In summer the offices are cooled by our own well water. For our buildings we use only pure materials like Portland cement or white limestone. I invented some of the building techniques, for ex-

ample the one for the floors. Instead of finishing the smoothed concrete floors with screed, we apply felt, on top of which comes squared timber followed by oaken parquet, which is then oiled and waxed. The result is a springy floor that is warm to the feet.

Edwin Kohl You said it. I invest in the comfort of the workplace. My employees are more content and efficient.

Edwin Kohl No, because our planning is very reduced, that is to say, we avoid superfluous architectural details. The saved costs go into the low-power technology.

Edwin Kohl I think it's fantastic, and it's just a pity that the requisite technology was not developed further before now, although we've known about it for twenty years.

Edwin Kohl Although producing heat by solar energy is so simple and efficient with parabolic trough technology. Today we've got direct current transmission lines, meaning infinite numbers of solar-thermal plants can be operated in the Sahara, and thanks to high-voltage direct-current transmission technology they no longer lose power.

Edwin Kohl E-mobility is my latest baby. I recently became the majority shareholder in the makers of the Mia electric car.

Edwin Kohl Well, of course I'll stay a pharmacist. I was originally on the lookout for an e-car for our reps and partner pharmacies in AVIE. And I wanted our trainees to have the incentive of driving an electric company car. The only project I found convincing was Murat Günak's Mia. But that's enough about me. What new projects are you working on, Mr. Dietz?

Ulrich Dietz I'm currently thinking intensively about a creative center I envisage building in Stuttgart. I want to gather together five hundred companies from future-oriented industry, from the one-man operation up to larger, established businesses. Experience tells me: the more forms of creativity meet up and mingle—from IT specialist, media expert, and energy scientist to artist, chef or hairdresser, for example—the greater the chances are for sustainable, profitable themes and products. As a first step we want to launch a "future fund" with a cash volume of two hundred million euros supplied by a small number of institutional investors and a large number of private investors. We plan to use the fund initially to develop several properties where companies—start-ups and existing operations—will be based. The interest shown by investors, among them pension funds, is unexpectedly high. The politicians are interested in our project too. Its strength lies in the fact that it is a closed system—similar to your own—a format that intermeshes both finances as well as the properties and the companies. We're still involved in the search for a suitable, if possible extraordinary, property or, if necessary, for suitable plots of land.

Edwin Kohl That's the kind of productivity enhancement we need. It's the only way to stay innovative.

Ulrich Dietz And, beyond that, also through a further exploitation of labor productivity. If we had more nursery schools with better staffing levels, the number of women in the workplace would increase by one third. The same is true of schools, which we can likewise integrate in our model. If we offer the appropriate infrastructure, we create attractive working conditions.

Edwin Kohl Very good: creativity concentrated in the way you describe lays a foundation for the future.

Ulrich Dietz Do you believe that the success of your company is due to your toughness and perseverance?

Edwin Kohl Absolutely. If you're convinced of a concept's potential, of its prospective profit margins, then you have to persevere until it's up and running.

Ulrich Dietz Considering our topic, I couldn't close the interview without inquiring after your own health. Are inventors healthier people?

Edwin Kohl I'll pass the question back to you.

Ulrich Dietz In my opinion, they are. What could be healthier than the joy of coming up with solutions for the benefit of human beings?

Edwin Kohl Exactly. It's enriching, and by no means only in the material sense, to see that what you do makes sense.

MONTJUIC
DEL BISBE

Claudia Llosa

"Believing in yourself is perhaps the origin of innovation."

Claudia Llosa

Born in Lima in 1976, the niece of the Peruvian writer Mario Vargas Llosa studied communications studies in her native city. In the late 1990s she moved to Madrid, where from 1998 to 2001 she studied film and television at the Escuela TAI arts school. At the time she began working on her first film script, *Madeinusa,* which she entered in the competition of the Havana International Film Festival in 2003 and promptly received the prize for the best original screenplay. That was followed by stipends and stays abroad, then in 2006 *Madeinusa,* coproduced by Llosa, had its premiere and won numerous prizes. *Milk of Sorrow* in 2009 was even more successful; among other prizes, it received the Golden Bear at the fifty-ninth Berlinale International Film Festival in Berlin.

In a narrow lane just a few steps away from the Gothic cathedral in Barcelona lies one of the most charming hotels in the city: the Neri. The lobby behind the walls of an eighteen-century urban palace is bright and tall; a giant green fan palm stands at the entrance to the stairs. Claudia Llosa walks through the glass door at a spirited pace, shakes her mane of hair, embraces us in a greeting, and proposes going up to the sunny roof terrace. Rather than choosing the recliners in this little oasis, we sit down at a table beneath dense foliage. A warm wind blows, and Llosa's bright, throaty voice effortlessly overpowers the shrieks of the children playing in the school below us. She speaks with an intuitive intelligence and ebullient joie de vivre, so it is no wonder we nearly miss our return flight.

Ulrich Dietz It's nice that we can meet in the center of Barcelona in such a tranquil place. I love this city with its special flair and southern atmosphere. Moreover Barcelona is one of the most creative cities in the world at the moment. Because we employ around seven hundred IT specialists in Spain, I am here six or seven times a year, and every time I am taken by it anew.

Claudia Llosa I also love Barcelona! It has been my adopted city for eight years now; I wrote my first screenplay, *Madeinusa*, here, got married, and gave birth to my son.

Ulrich Dietz Do you miss your native country, Peru, sometimes?

Claudia Llosa All the time. That's why I go there two or three times a year to see my family. Do you know Lima?

Ulrich Dietz No, unfortunately, not yet. But my sister Sabine is there regularly. Together with her husband and five other friends, they founded a nonprofit organization, El Pueblo Unido—Solidarität mit Lateinamerika (The people united: Solidarity with Latin America), and for nearly twenty years she has been supporting a school for children on the streets in Cajamarca. They bring the donations themselves, so they don't fall into the wrong hands.

Claudia Llosa That's great! How did she end up in our country, of all places?

Ulrich Dietz Some of her fellow students at the university were Peruvian, and they told her about the economic and political situation, which was very harsh at the time. Has the situation improved in the meantime?

Claudia Llosa It's a laborious and difficult process. As you know, Peru was terrorized by the Maoist guerrilla movement Sendero Luminoso for decades. The population had to endure a horrible civil-war in which nearly seventy thousand people were killed.

Ulrich Dietz Which brings us to your film *La Teta asustada*, called *Milk of Sorrow* in English, which won the Golden Bear at the Berlinale in 2009. It touched me like few other films I have seen. You succeed in conveying emotions directly. The film communicates very intensely the soul of a country and its people. It's one thing when James Cameron makes a film like *Avatar* with the most modern technology and a budget of millions. But what you have managed to do with a little over a million dollars is tell a half-documentary, half-mythical/

fictional story with powerful and clear images— that is creative! As an engineer, what fascinated me especially is how sharp and precise your perspective is—and at the same time poetic!

Claudia Llosa Thank you, that's nice to hear! The basic idea of *La Teta asustada* is to narrate the collective trauma, whose victims include so many people, especially farmers from the desperately poor province of Ayacucho, in the Andean highlands. These people were totally neglected by different governments throughout our history. In the 1980s and 1990s, there were murders, torture, and brutal mass rapes in nearly half of the country. I read hundreds of reports that were almost unbearable and studied scholarly papers such as the one by the North American anthropologist Kimberly Theidon.

Ulrich Dietz What people do to one another is often incomprehensible. Your famous uncle Mario Vargas Llosa wrote about it in his book *Death in the Andes.*

Claudia Llosa Exactly. In 1996 he received the Peace Prize of the German Book Trade for it, among others. He has always been politically engaged and has a tremendous courage of his convictions, which I admire about him.

Ulrich Dietz Did he inspire you to make films? Or was it rather another relative, the film director and producer Luis Llosa? You seem to come from a very creative family.

Claudia Llosa Yes, there are a lot of artists in our family, not least my mother. She is a video artist, and now the art director of my films. But films were not my focus originally; literature was. I started writing poems at the age of six. Until recently, however, I did not have much contact with my uncle Mario. He is not the person I have to thank for becoming a film director; Agnès Varda is.

Ulrich Dietz The great Belgian filmmaker and *Grande Dame* of the Nouvelle Vague.

Claudia Llosa More precisely, her works, since I have never met her personally. I remember exactly when I saw her for the first time in one of her documentary fictions. She seemed so vital to me, so beautiful with all her wrinkles! Her radiance and presence impressed me deeply. Agnès Varda does what she believes without concessions. I wanted to do the same.

Ulrich Dietz I also sense in you the very energy you are describing.

Claudia Llosa Believing in yourself is the most important thing. Perhaps it is even the origin of innovation?

Ulrich Dietz Because faith moves mountains, as we say? Certainly, a powerful faith, unconditional will, can make the impossible possible.

Claudia Llosa I have given some thought to what the new means to me. I like the word new. But I prefer the word "unique." For me, "unique" is when someone contributes his or her personality without reservation and honestly.

Ulrich Dietz Do you mean who is authentic? That word also comes up in several of the other interviews in the book. More and more, I have the impression that the authenticity of a person, his or her fidelity to himself or herself, contains both elements: the new and the original.

Claudia Llosa For me, "innovative" is the same as being unique. Daring to be yourself. Dedicating yourself to everything you do. But that only works if you are not obsessed with the idea of uniqueness.

Ulrich Dietz Because then it would just be an attitude? Probably the hardest thing is remaining honest to oneself. Because you have no distance from yourself.

Claudia Llosa Moreover, everyone wants to be loved, and for that most people make too many compromises. But anyone who wants to create something new has to have the courage to fail.

Ulrich Dietz That's another key sentence that has occurred repeatedly in our conversations. And a third point is important: If you or I were to cease offering the new for just one moment in the unbelievable competition in our respective fields, we would not be successful.

Claudia Llosa That's true!

Ulrich Dietz The question is what makes a product new. The authenticity of which we just spoke is crucial. Anyone who acts authentically is free. You don't even need a lot of money to create something new. I think your success was also helped by the fact you had little to lose.

Claudia Llosa Sure, when you are young, you are more willing to pursue crazy ideas. As the potato in *La Teta asustada*.

Ulrich Dietz A radical image. How did you come up with the idea?

Claudia Llosa Translated literally, *La Teta asustada* means "The Frightened Teat," but in English the film is called *Milk of Sorrow*. My heroine, Fausta, is the daughter of a mother who was raped during Sendero Luminoso's reign of terror. She is the child of this violation, and she literally took in her mother's trauma and suffering with her mother's milk. It has transferred to the daughter, and she has to live with it. In order to protect herself against this ignominy she finds embarrassing, Fausta puts a potato in her vagina. I wanted to show as graphically as possible what someone who does not want to be a victim under any circumstances is capable of. That was the challenge. And under no circumstances did I want to show my people in the role of victims. On the contrary, my film was meant to be a contribution to us Peruvians gradually regaining our self-esteem, so that we would learn to appreciate ourselves.

Ulrich Dietz It achieved that goal. In Peru, 250,000 people saw *La Teta asustada*.

Claudia Llosa A great thing for a country like this, whose film industry produces only about a dozen films a year. Usually only big productions from the United States have attendance figures like that in our country.

Ulrich Dietz What was the premiere like?

Claudia Llosa An overwhelming celebration! It was held in Manchay, the village where we filmed. Everyone came; everyone saw the film on a giant screen in the center of the market square. People danced and cried "Viva Manchay" and "Viva *La Teta asustada*." Everyone was so proud! That's why it was so important that the film won prizes and became so popular. Its worldwide success returned to Peru as a message that it pays to fight for a better future.

Ulrich Dietz What do you see as Peru's future?

Claudia Llosa We are at a very promising point, since now there is a more stable middle class. More and more people have a modest prosperity to defend. Now they are fighting for their income, their living space, their security and freedom. Our hope for a better future is becoming more tangible. That is a new, very positive state of consciousness for us.

Ulrich Dietz Also a more fearless one?

Claudia Llosa That too. Although we are far from having lost our fears. We still don't trust our new reality entirely. But this degree of instability also has something positive, since it keeps us alert.

Ulrich Dietz It's a balancing act. In a certain way, we are constantly crossing boundaries, seeing a balance between opportunities and risks, guarantees and uncertainties, regardless of whether we are in technology or the arts.

Claudia Llosa That's why every new project is a beginning that requires total commitment just like the first time.

Ulrich Dietz Routine is poison for innovation. You have to surprise constantly, although not only the expectations one has of oneself, but also the expectations of the audience, or in my case of the clients, are always increasing. The crucial thing is exploring new, broader dimensions.

Claudia Llosa Even a tiny step, a small shift, suffices. For example, when you find an unexpected perspective that is not yet visible to others. When I was young, I always thought I had to descend deep into some abysses inside me in order to be creative. But I am a happy girl. I do have dark places, but I believe empathy is the key to creativity. The ability to empathize with others, to sympathize with them, to connect to them. Everyone who has this gift of empathy is creative, no matter whether they are teachers, scientists, carpenters, managers, or artists.

Ulrich Dietz A remarkable insight! Already in your first film, *Madeinusa*, you had this special ability to empathize of which you are speaking. And that film also won prizes, including best original screenplay in Havana and the grand prize of film critics in Rotterdam. What is it about?

Claudia Llosa It is another story of being liberated to be oneself. Madeinusa is a fourteen-year-old, very pretty girl from a remote village in the Andes, Manayaycuna, where every year between Good Friday and Easter Sunday archaic, orgiastic rituals are celebrated. A foreigner who ends up in the region falls in love with Madeinusa. Her name is, by the way, like Darling or JohnFKennedy, a very common first name in these regions, where most of the people are illiterate. And Manayaycuna, the name I invented for the village, means something like "enclosed village" in Quechua, the language of the natives there. In any case, Madeinusa sees the photographer Salvador as her salvation, as a way to escape finally the rigid, misogynistic rules of the village community. The film resulted from my need to understand my homeland, Peru, better. The richness of its traditions and its superstitious religious practices, which for some time have been mixing in such bizarre ways with Western American pop influences. This mixture characterizes our *cultura chicha*.

Ulrich Dietz Another thing that distinguishes your films is your sense of humor, which pops up again and again. Do Peruvians like comedy?

Claudia Llosa Oh yes! In Peru, men in particular are constantly making fun of one another. We women crack fewer jokes, but we kid and like to laugh. We Peruvians are especially good at laughing at ourselves.

Ulrich Dietz A wonderful ability that makes life easier. Is there something like a moment when a film is born?

Claudia Llosa In the beginning, everything is diffuse. First I have to find the atmosphere. Then I write one scene, then another. It is not a linear process; the sequences only begin to interweave gradually. In the meantime, however, I try as early as possible to work out a crude structure, a framework, so that I don't get trapped in the labyrinth of my own ideas.

Ulrich Dietz Realizing the new takes time. Although it helps when one is constantly involved in a creative process as you are.

Claudia Llosa It works if you can concentrate on one thing. Until now, that was simple for me, but in the meantime I am showered with invitations and requests from all over the world. I am just learning to say no.

Ulrich Dietz Establishing preferences is important. And the best thing about it is that you rarely miss anything when you say no! How did you discover Magaly Solier, the sensational female lead in your films?

Claudia Llosa Magaly is a rare natural talent with an unerring intuition that always leads her to do the right thing. She wrote three songs from my first film, *Madeinusa,* herself, and composed the music for the songs that I wrote for *La Teta asustada.*

Ulrich Dietz Even though she is self-taught?

Claudia Llosa Yes. I met her when I was traveling through churches in the region at Easter to find a very specific image of Christ. As I was leaving the church in Ayacucho, Magaly was sitting on the steps and charmed me with her unusual beauty, her high cheekbones, brown eyes, and bronze complexion. It was a great stroke of luck.

Ulrich Dietz Are you also searching for beauty in your films?

Claudia Llosa Yes, definitely. I often think about beauty. Its ideals have changed greatly again and again over the course of millennia. Even so, there is universal, timeless agreement about what beauty is. I'm searching for a new beauty beyond our conventions and standards. A beauty we immediately recognize, even though it's new.

Ulrich Dietz Do you mean a beauty beyond perfection and artificial symmetry?

Claudia Llosa Yes. I believe I am searching for a beauty of grace. The beauty of the soul.

Wayne McGregor

"It is important to generate opportunities to make mistakes."

Wayne McGregor

As a child he loved computer games and admired John Travolta. As a teenager he danced in clubs and imitated choppy "robot moves" with his wiry body. Born in Stockport, England, in 1970 the artist started his career with that same turbo energy and always casual grace in performance. He studied choreography and semiotics in Leeds and at the José Limon School in New York. In 1992 he founded his company, Wayne McGregor | Random Dance, named in allusion to British biologist Richard Dawkins's theory of random mutation. Since 2000, McGregor has been experimenting with behavioral research; since 2006 he has been the first contemporary choreographer of the Royal Ballet in London. The artist has received numerous prizes for more than ninety productions, including *Yantra* and *Outlier* in 2010, and is considered a revolutionary of contemporary dance.

Where does one make plans to meet a choreographer if not in his studio? Wayne McGregor meets us at the stage entrance to the Royal Ballet in London. "Nice to see you," smiles the busy man and beams from silvery gray eyes. He leads us through narrow, winding corridors to an elevator; dancers walk toward us; he embraces them—no question that he is a star here. Because his dressing room is the only quiet place, we sit down for our conversation amid mirrors, leotards, and ballet slippers. Books are stacked on the filing cabinet; whenever the artist finds a free minute, he reads. He sits up ramrod straight on a stool: "Let's start; we have exactly fifty minutes." But in the end he takes time for long answers, speaking in a bright voice, accompanying his sentences with flowing, rhythmical gestures with his arms and hands. McGregor shows us how thinking becomes body language.

Ulrich Dietz I must confess that as an engineer I don't really know what motivates a famous choreographer like you. Contemporary dance is not especially close to me.

Wayne McGregor Why not? You have a body. That makes you perfectly qualified.

Ulrich Dietz Well, fine. I consider you innovative because you radically transcend the boundaries of your discipline—for example, by cooperating with neuroscientists. Why do you do this?

Wayne McGregor Because I want to discover and understand how the mind and the body interact as an interconnected whole. My company Wayne McGregor | Random Dance and I have been experimenting intensely for nearly ten years with cognitive scientists who study this interaction. In classical ballet and modern dance, technique is still focused on physical training to the point of perfection. People concern themselves with virtuosity and controlling the body—the mind is essentially ignored. I completely reject this separation of mind and body. Fortunately, science is increasingly demonstrating how absurd this split is, and addressing a notion of embodied cognition far more seriously. We are finding out more and more about how our imagination integrates emotion, sensation, memory, movement, and language. We understand that there are techniques not only for training the body, but also for enhancing creativity and stimulating a richer imagination.

Ulrich Dietz How?

Wayne McGregor Artists often claim they work instinctively. This is only partially true. This so-called creative instinct is always integrated with our cognitive faculties.

Ulrich Dietz A concrete example would be helpful.

Wayne McGregor Dance is essentially a collaborative art form, usually it requires other individuals to participate in the generation of the work. A choreographic process is an ideal example of distributed cognition. In a project at the University of California, San Diego, we investigated how ideas are disseminated or distributed within a team. This led to some very interesting insights about how the creative process evolves which in turn shaped our next creative process. We looked at some seminal questions: during a making process which parts of an idea are retained by the group (or individual) and which parts are dropped? What mental models do we each develop when we improvise together? What forms of communication do we use to share, transform and vary the ideas, and how are gesture, verbal language and sound utilized to embody the concepts? With a greater understanding of these issues we can better distinguish between the choreography of images and scenes. This can even give rise to new techniques.

Ulrich Dietz Can anyone learn that? Even someone who has no dance training?

Wayne McGregor Definitely. When I work with young dancers, the first thing I do is encourage them to trust their bodies. They should experience how wonderful it is to dance. How it feels to jump, to stretch out, to turn, to walk, to run. They can learn flawless *pliés* later. First you have to awaken the passion for dance; everything else will follow. Then you can seed these new creative techniques so they start to generate and choreograph their own dances—they find their own expressive voice rather than imitating one, and rediscover themselves quite literally through dance.

Ulrich Dietz Can people of any age manage this passion?

Wayne McGregor Of course, it doesn't depend on age. More and more adults are attending dancing classes in their free time; there are dance shows on television with public casting sessions, and thousands of people register in the hope of being selected. In United Kingdom schools, dance is now the second most popular sport outside of football, not least because the government is strongly championing it. But for me, the creative aspects of dance making are the key to self-discovery—it's the integration of the visceral thrill of moving with the flight of the imagination. I believe the need to feel the body is increasing as our world becomes more virtual.

Ulrich Dietz Do you reject virtual spheres?

Wayne McGregor On the contrary. I am fascinated by cyberspace, technology and virtual spheres and often embrace these aspects in my work. But I also know that the body and its specific intelligence and imagination cannot be replaced. We each have a unique body through which we perceive ourselves, and others in the world. The body is our membrane, our filter to everything around us, our sense maker.

Ulrich Dietz Where do you start when you choreograph? With the music?

Wayne McGregor Many choreographers do indeed get their inspiration from music and why not, it is such a deep mine of possibility. Traditionally there is often a hierarchy in which music comes first, followed by the body, and I have always tried to break out of such patterns. For me, the impetus for choreography can be anything: a melody, a rhythm, yes, but more frequently, an object, a philosophy, a scientific fact, even software. I am interested in accessing the full range.

Wayne McGregor Hmmm, not an easy question. I think for our audiences, meaning emerges from their active participation in the viewing. They are not looking to be simply entertained, but they are looking to navigate the work themselves and engage with the questions it presents. For me, dance has not only an emotional dimension but also an intellectual one. Part of the attraction to the work, and by definition the repulsion for some, is the actual physical vocabulary the dancers execute, with its often abrupt, distorted, torsioned movement that seems alien to the body. But dysfunctional, damaged, traumatized bodies have always interested me a lot, precisely because they are not stereotyped. Learning to understand the beauty of this "other" body language is something I consider very important to appreciating the work. For this you have to be open to a body misbehaving, a body not obeying the conventional rules of dancing and for some this is too far an aesthetic stretch.

Wayne McGregor Yes. There are so many prejudices. One of them is to assume science and emotion have no points of contact. It's just the opposite: without emotions there is no reason. As a choreographer, I try to create an experience for the audience in which emotions and ideas are evoked. I do not manipulate them to read the dance in a certain way, as happens, for example, in traditional narrative ballet. I offer a landscape that is charged with qualities, images, feeling, emotions, patterns, raw physicality and hopefully surprises from which sense emerges. Audiences have to do some of the work in recognizing these clues, and allowing them to provoke responses inside themselves rather than waiting for the "story" to be told.

Wayne McGregor I want to reveal their own creativity to them. Being an audience member is a creative act. Creativity doesn't rest on the stage. As such, as audience members we can develop our creative instincts, our creative responses to the work and go on a journey of discovery in the same way the art makers can. But to do this you have to recognize firstly how you watch, and then actively challenge yourself, to watch differently, more openly. Creativity in watching is a fluid competence audiences can acquire to feed themselves, like learning a foreign language. Many people—including audience members as well as artists—associate creativity with some kind of abstract, mystical, intangible force that just "is" either you fall into the camp of someone who is creative or you do not. Full stop. Worse, for many, the notion of creativity is something they find intimidating, threatening and alien. Yet we all perform extremely creative acts every day. Everyone has very real, creative competences which, once recognized, can be trained!

Wayne McGregor There are many creative competences including: encouraging active problem solving, developing an independence of thought and functioning, learning new ways of extracting information from things, using the body as an object to think with, exploring alternative decision making etc. These are competences we are actively training through our use of creative imagery tools and techniques in the studio. But it is just as important to understand how to generate opportunities to make mistakes. Creativity often comes at the point where you make a mistake. Then you make another, and another, and another…and at some point you suddenly make something original. At school we are usually taught to do the right thing, give the correct response not the original thing; our creative impulses can be destroyed. That can include the ability to think independently. Or to deal with a task differently today from how you did it yesterday. Creative minds understand their habitual patterns and seek to disrupt them, or at least continually invent new ones.

Wayne McGregor It is a complicated, long term project. We are pursuing several lines of overlapping enquiry trying to find out what kinesthetic intelligence really is. For example, for one project we are constructing software from basic choreographic elements—if you will, an agent that speaks a choreographic language. This software is not supposed to dance but rather to produce choreographic thinking that is completely independent of dance, which means it might contribute to design thinking in other fields such as architecture.

 With the objective of translating one form of creative intelligence into another—a kind of translation and simultaneous networking?

Wayne McGregor Exactly. This agent is able to make decisions and find solutions. For my next choreographies, I will be taking the software into the studio with me. We'll see what happens.

Ulrich Dietz How do you want to integrate this software into your choreography?

Wayne McGregor That's an adventure we still have to confront.

Ulrich Dietz Your company is open to these expeditions?

Wayne McGregor Absolutely. I have been working with most of the dancers for many years, and they have each contributed essentially and immeasurably to the direction we are now taking. In the beginning there was some hesitancy as we found our unique way of communicating with the cognitive scientists—we all needed to learn each other's languages, at least in part. We were all breaking new ground and conscious of the difficulties in this. But as we persevered we have found the collaboration easier, enlightening and terribly fulfilling.

Ulrich Dietz Do the scientists profit from it as well?

Wayne McGregor I hope so. I think the scientists gain new insights in their special fields. All of the scientists we work with are trying to understand aspects of embodiment. Are you familiar with Wii from the Japanese company Nintendo?

Ulrich Dietz Of course, it makes it simpler and more varied to play different video games.

Wayne McGregor It is the simple version of a technology that transforms physical activity—that is, real movements—into movements on the screen.

Ulrich Dietz Which "embodies" them.

Wayne McGregor Exactly. The subject is hot at the moment. The point is to interact physically with technology. Technology is supposed to become part of the body, to fuse with it in a sense.

Ulrich Dietz The applications for industry are gigantic, not just in the areas of sports and games.

Wayne McGregor Right. Embodiment has potential for generally interacting with our technological environments in more of an intimate way. There are potential military uses as well. Gesture recognition and the ability to recognize "physical signatures", or the uniqueness of an individual's movement may be a very potent tool in the future.

Ulrich Dietz Isn't that a little strange, even threatening, as well?

Wayne McGregor Not if we use these new technologies responsibly.

Ulrich Dietz So, like most pioneers, you see new technological possibilities as positive?

Wayne McGregor Yes, you can't predict their usefulness. Look at the Internet and its radical impact on the world in a decade. Technology affords us opportunities that don't yet exist. This is extremely enticing for art making. Technology has a massive impact on how, who and where work is made and that in itself can be very liberating. It totally makes a difference whether I develop choreography live for stage, or if I create a work to be experienced simultaneously through live streaming via a screen. It changes your creative decision-making process, the way you fundamentally move, the way you think. This disruption to the normal practice results in interesting diversions—imaginative invention. This constant feedback effect via technology changes how I choreograph my next piece, and the next piece after that. It's a recurring and constant process of exchange in which something new always emerges. Unfortunately, so often the big lyric theatres and critics are nervous of the "new", and typically risk averse—they almost want you to replicate your last hit.

Ulrich Dietz That's the trouble in the business world as well. Usually the same applications and approaches are repeated rather than risking something new. Far too many companies are guided by the market rather than thinking ahead and creating their own new markets.

Wayne McGregor Exactly. I believe it's difficult in any sphere to break out of the existing framework. One of the keys to doing so, is to know how to make decisions. You have to analyze the way to make atypical decisions. You have to cultivate that ability.

Ulrich Dietz Because that is the crux of creativity and innovativeness?

Wayne McGregor Innovativeness is a by-product of creativity. You can't simply decide: now I will make an innovative work. But you can improve your creative facilities that in turn provoke potential novelty in your imagination that then inspires invention. Innovation may result by chance in the process, but you can't call it up in a linear way. But for me, part of the joy in creating is placing yourself at the center of unknowing. It's a place where I have very few of the answers but too many of the questions!

Ulrich Dietz A favorite ploy. How important the area of innovation is. Most people deny it.

Wayne McGregor You said it!

Ulrich Dietz What is your next big project?

Wayne McGregor The Big Dance 2012 in time for the London Olympics. We will work with more than ten thousand children and young people who will each create and perform their own dances in Trafalgar Square.

Ulrich Dietz That sounds like fun. Are they budding professionals?

Wayne McGregor Some of them, but on the whole we prefer working with young people who haven't had any formal training. They are not so obsessed with the prescribed "rules" then. They are freer.

Ulrich Dietz Don't dance studios teach according to standards? For many people, it is about having a fit, shapely body, and not so much about creativity.

Wayne McGregor Unfortunately there is a huge gap opening up between dance as exclusively physical activity and dance as an expressive art form.

Ulrich Dietz We are confronted with the same dilemma with the teaching subjects at school. The curriculum follows rigid prescriptions. And sports are always neglected. Dance classes are even rarer.

Wayne McGregor It is upsetting how standardized our everyday dealings with our bodies have become. Many people only really pay attention to their bodies when something goes wrong. Otherwise, the body simply functions beyond our perception of it, but very much in the realm of normalized activity. In some ways new technology is helping bridge that gap. Interactive video games like *Guitar Hero* or the Wii are encouraging bodies to do things they don't normally encounter—stretching themselves beyond the functional. These new embodied technologies may provide a key to accessing less sedentary lives. Here technology can help us become more famil-

iar with our bodies—a contradictory thought to the usual technology-equals-less-familiarity argument.

Ulrich Dietz How was it in your case?

Wayne McGregor I was very active physically from a young age and played a lot of sport, was always swimming, climbing, and dancing too. But I also belong to the first generation that grew up with computers and spent hours on my Spectrum typing in basic programming to make a ball cross the screen! So it's really only logical that I now travel regularly to San Diego to work with scientists to develop choreographic thinking tools.

Ulrich Dietz Perhaps resulting in applications that make people more creative. Could these tools also be applied to medicine?

Wayne McGregor Perhaps yes. Already cognitive "signals"—the act of thinking up, or thinking down have been harnessed to play games on computer, or to animate inanimate objects. The potential benefit for this type of research on people with physical paralysis, for example, may be rather powerful. Cognitive therapies may well be advanced with a richer understanding of embodiment theory, embedding the concept of "oneness"—the interconnected and inseparable functioning of the mind and body in new treatments. It's a rich territory to be explored.

Ulrich Dietz Several years ago you built a house with a large atelier and dance studio on the island of Lamu off the coast of Kenya. Is that your refuge?

Wayne McGregor In part. Lamu is an archipelago of islands in the Indian Ocean just off the east coast of Kenya. Lamu has a rich cultural and historical tradition reaching back to the ninth century and as a UNESCO World Heritage Site is the oldest living Swahili town in Kenya. The islands can only be reached by boat. There I read, listen to music, do research, give free rein to my thoughts and ideas. But I also invite artists: dancers, musicians, writers. It is inspiring for everyone.

Ulrich Dietz What is your vision?

Wayne McGregor To be open to new possibilities and ever curious. Those fields of research outside the art world bear rich pickings for experimentation and knowledge transfer, and that to be creative is a resource we all can share.

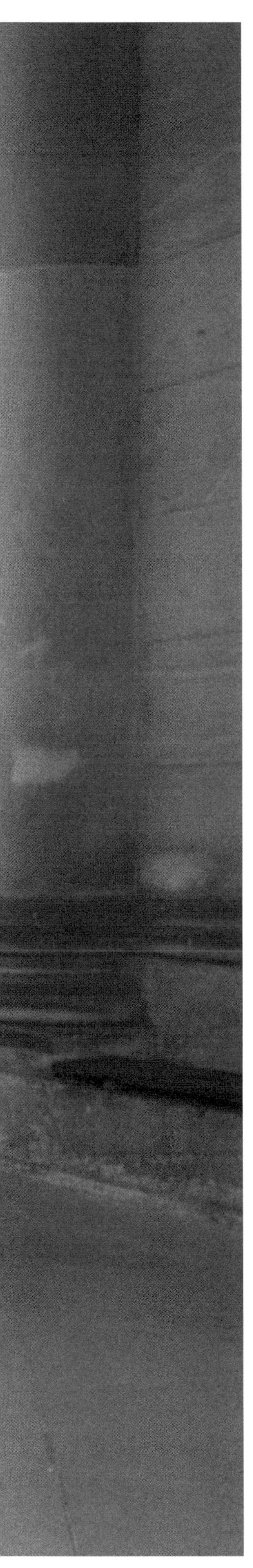

Paulus Neef

"Nothing ventured, nothing gained."

Paulus Neef

Through the Pixelpark agency, which he cofounded in 1991 with two friends, Paulus Neef became the star of the new economy in Europe. Born in Gütersloh in 1960 to a German father and a Spanish mother, he studied publicity and marketing and then worked as a media consultant. He built up the digital television station SK4 and was responsible for marketing and acquisition for Cinepool. Pixelpark AG went public in 1999 with an issue price of fifteen euros a share. In 2001 he had 1,200 employees and shares were 385 euros. But a complete crash soon followed. In 2002 Neef lost his job, but not his founder's gene. Indefatigable, he is involved in several companies today and just founded MAMA, an ethical venture-capital-company that wants to support start-up entrepreneurs in the area of sustainability.

The Café Einstein in the Mitte district of Berlin is the daily haunt of
Paulus Neef, a Berliner by adoption. Paulus reserved a table in the back
room to ensure us a quiet place. As friends and colleagues for many
years, we pat each other on the shoulder and embrace warmly as a greeting. Everything all right? Great! Neef is a man who knows the highs
and lows of entrepreneurship like few others. With his agency Pixelpark,
he tapped the pulse of the time, and with his new company, MAMA,
he is betting on sustainability. He can teach us the meaning of audacity:
never giving up. After three hours of intense discussion, we feel hungry.
Schnitzel and cucumber salad for everyone, please!

Ulrich Dietz Paulus, how would you react if I said, "You have to protect yourself from your own creativity?"

Paulus Neef What do you mean? Do you want to annoy me?

Ulrich Dietz In our company we have an innovation-management filter system with which we check new business ideas against their realizability and economic potential. This even occasionally filters out business ideas I myself have developed, and that would have been important to me. Although it doesn't entirely prevent flops and mistaken investments, at least it makes them less likely. Have you ever wondered if your old Internet company Pixelpark would have been more successful with a good controlling system?

Paulus Neef I think that trying to protect someone from his own creativity is almost dangerous. Because I believe that inventors and entrepreneurs always need to make a radical break with tradition and classical business modes. If you want to be creative, you sometimes have to dare to wipe the slate clean. Bringing in the realizability filter too soon can be a big mistake. New things often come about from an apparent by-product or a marginal theme.

Ulrich Dietz That may be, but not necessarily.

Paulus Neef I'll give you an example. Nokia was originally involved in rubber processing and produced tyres and rubber boots. Through the principle of trial and error, and a lot of daring, at some point the founders landed on the cell phone. A development like this would have been impossible through normal business practice. Creativity cannot be measured like lengths of wire. It needs a free zone it can flow in.

Ulrich Dietz I agree with you there. It goes without saying that creativity needs the proper environment in which to develop, and very different kinds of specialists, whose ideas can come together in attraction, repulsion and combination. What I'm trying to get at is the question of how to realize a new product or service in a sustainable and economically successful way? If you have it too easy in the beginning, isn't the danger of failure greater than if you need to overcome resistance, and constantly check and question your ideas? An idea often only becomes a success in the second or third round, after being modified. You know what happened when we wanted to start a digital magazine around five years ago. It was supposed to bring high-quality print media on to the Internet and link them with consumer services like shopping addresses or other information. We spoke to a lot of different publishers at the time, but they were all afraid of implementing the idea.

Paulus Neef They were afraid of being cannibalized. Today we'd have a greater chance of success, now that print-media circulation is falling and they're frantically looking for alternatives.

Ulrich Dietz We were ahead of our time?

Paulus Neef Obviously. Today publishers are starting to think about charging a fee for premium content. And they're doing exactly what we suggested to them back then: marketing their key content in a synergetic way!

Ulrich Dietz The *Wall Street Journal* is still one of the few publications that earns money from Web subscriptions. Perhaps the company performances in the print media need to get even worse before they're prepared to exploit the possibilities of the Internet. The worlds are still very separate, and there's too little understanding of how you can earn money creatively on the Internet.

Paulus Neef Because most people can't think in parallel structures.

Ulrich Dietz And because a lot of technologies need much more time to develop than people think is possible in the euphoric discovery phase. In the 1980s I had the wonderful opportunity of taking part in the development of what were then trailblazing CO_2 lasers for metalwork. It took ten years before they were good enough to earn any money, and above all until they could be used for a variety of purposes. But then the investments paid off. I think it's decisive to become occupied with new themes or technologies for as long as you need in order to master the field. Stamina and patience are the be all and end all. Profitability is secondary to begin with.

Paulus Neef I completely agree with you!

Ulrich Dietz You can only develop something really new if you do something from experience. The iPhone is the best example. The technologies were already there—the new thing was the design and ease of operation. The product has altered the lifestyle of an entire generation. I found something you said once very important in this context: "I'm excited by making connections where they didn't previously exist. Building up added value at this interface. This is how innovation comes about."

Paulus Neef That's my leitmotif. I think it applies to all areas, from research to craft to art. We're all blind specialists, in a way. Focused on our own areas of knowledge. But our compulsion towards specialization and perfection fixes us in a single direction, and more and more details, for too long. That's why we're usually too late in starting to network intelligently and looking at the periphery.

Ulrich Dietz That sounds a bit too simple to me. Among other things, specialists have the advantage of being able to make exclusive use of niches. We, for example, do this with IT services for the financial sector. We've become one of the world's most well-known providers through many years of improvement and a deep understanding of our clients' business processes. This gives us a clear competitive advantage and a greater resistance to crises and market fluctuation.

Paulus Neef There's still no evidence to the contrary. Next to well-known brands like yours there are thousands of equal quality that are unknown. And why? Because they don't market themselves. One of my friends at the UBS looks after so-called small caps—firms with a stock-exchange capitalization of under a hundred million euros—for an investment fund. He's very successful in picking out the undervalued champions—companies that are world-market leaders, yet largely unknown. And so he can support them cheaply, make them better known with the invested funds and improve their market value. Companies like these are rarely found in big cities, by the way, but in more remote areas.

Ulrich Dietz For example St. Georgen in the Black Forest. That's innovative economics, with the proviso that the exit strategy of the funds—which want their money back with interest at some point – is also attractive for the affected companies. Many companies, particularly small or medium-sized family firms, aren't interested in being "blown upwards" because they're concerned about their long term independence. And there's another thing you shouldn't forget: the higher you fly, the harder you fall. Think about corporate development during the time of the Internet bubble at the turn of the millennium.

Paulus Neef But if some do want to expand into a dynamically expanding market, it can be the right way of going about things. You have to carefully weigh up whether you want a maximum monetization or, like us, you primarily want to create and renew in a sustainable way.

Ulrich Dietz We're entrepreneurs. We do what we do because we enjoy it. Of course we have to make money, but that's not the focus in the beginning. People are continually asking me why we don't sell GFT—but what would I do then? Sit in the sun drinking red wine?

Paulus Neef We do that now sometimes! Aren't the technological developments in our globalized world incredibly exciting? Particularly in the overlapping areas of media, Internet and telecommunications. As someone who thinks entrepreneurially you have to seize the chance and develop business models accordingly.

Ulrich Dietz Absolutely. And, as Hermann Hesse put it so well, we fell for the magic of the beginning. This is unfortunately quite happily argued away by the sceptics of this world. Creativity should instead be supported and developed from the very beginning. Children shouldn't only be drilled in learning content; we have to strengthen their love of discovery.

Paulus Neef Can you learn creativity? For me it's the ability to deal with disparate worlds that apparently have nothing to do with one another. As a German Spaniard I grew up in two cultures. I inherited the impulsive temperament of my mother and the analytical understanding of my father. I experience this as a valuable gain. Perhaps the mixture makes you even more creative. On the other hand, I think you can go much further if you learn how to continually simplify things. That's a form of creativity in itself.

Ulrich Dietz You're right. In my case I've always had a penchant for developing business ideas from new things. I founded my first company at the age of nineteen. We made exploded diagrams of technical instruments. In those days I also learned how to draw with computer systems and realized that their handling was far too complicated. Years later, and after many thousands of hours at the drawing board, we developed a software for engineers with which it was easy to create diagrams of machines and instruments. Its operation was as intuitive as with Apple. That was the basis of GFT.

Paulus Neef That's typical for an entrepreneur: nothing ventured, nothing gained, that's the point. At GFT you've always come up with innovations before competitors even started thinking along similar lines. With me it's the same: I'd rather do something than not do it. It is a sense of unrest that continually drives me on to new things. In the meantime I have some experience in opening up new territories, and I can recognize problems earlier on and correct them sooner. But some dangers you can't predict—things that lie outside your own influence, like the financial crisis, for example.

Ulrich Dietz That's right, and yet the outstanding companies are conspicuous for being able to get through these crises because, apart from their good liquidity, they're also active in different markets and in many countries. It certainly protects you, even during a crisis, if you're the best in a niche market. As it says in the Bible, crises repeat themselves about every seven years. The last one was in 2001, and then came the collapse of Lehman Brothers in autumn 2008. When I founded GFT in 1987 we were in recession, which I hadn't realized. That's why—to finally answer your question about the qualities of the born entrepreneur—I think that the motivation shouldn't be primarily monetary. The entrepreneur has to want to risk making a start!

Paulus Neef He has to passionately want something new. I think that every company is founded from a deep need. I founded mine with two thousand euros, so it was absolutely necessary to convince other people about my vision. This would have been out of the question without the utmost enthusiasm for what I was doing.

Ulrich Dietz And without the famous beginner's luck of the naive.

Paulus Neef That's true. If I had imagined what I was going to come up against, I would never have started. But I was as fearless as a child—and protected for that very reason.

Ulrich Dietz It was exactly the same with me. If I'd known the risks beforehand, I wouldn't have taken a single step in the direction of self-employment.

Paulus Neef And the amazing thing is, you don't blank out this other side. It simply isn't there!

Ulrich Dietz You're describing the principle that artists and researchers work from. They exclude what's around them as much as possible in order to free their energies entirely for their ideas. Like most of us, including me, you have experienced reversals in the course of your career. Were you discouraged, or were they an incentive to do things better next time?

Paulus Neef I struggled, I went through the highs and lows, and I realized that life goes on. That made me more serene.

Ulrich Dietz What was the worst day of your professional life?

Paulus Neef I can't really answer that question head on. The worst thing was the feeling that Pixelpark had gone past its best. To see that from now on things could only go to the dogs. It wasn't just me. Lots of people in the New Economy suddenly stopped getting orders in 2002. At first you hope the situation will get better soon, you don't dismiss any staff, you have to go on outwardly playing the hero. But I increasingly had the sense that we were heading for a total disaster. It was a dreadful feeling. The fear of failure was the worst. I didn't go against things in time. Today I'd do it differently.

Ulrich Dietz The greatest difficulty is the awareness of having to make changes that will be uncomfortable for everyone involved. I'm thinking of times that were difficult for me, and there were a few. I always dealt with them like with a painful dental treatment. I endured them. Always with the thought that it would be over at some point. What else can you do but work even harder at getting back to better times? Of course the best thing would be not to get into such a situation in the first place. Actually there are always early indicators as to whether a product or a service will soon become obsolete. That's why it's important to spot the trends as early as possible, to draw the appropriate conclusions and then to work with all your might on their implementation with the support of as many people as possible.

Paulus Neef I'm thinking of the music industry. As long as a decade ago CD sales started falling. But even the industry's market leaders overslept the triumphal march of the download portals, because they didn't want to endanger their hierarchical star structures and their party-life-is-easy mentality.

Ulrich Dietz The great economist Joseph Schumpeter described what you're talking about as the fear of creative destruction: the fear of destroying an existing, still-functioning business model in order to build up a sustainable but as yet unknown one.

Paulus Neef Significantly, the innovation of iTunes didn't come from the music industry, but from a computer manufacturer, an outsider!

Ulrich Dietz Yet you can only survive these crises if you're open to this creative destruction. I'm thinking of the example of the frog: if you throw one into boiling water, it'll hop out again immediately. But if you put one in cold water and slowly heat it up to forty degrees, the creature just goes on sitting there while its proteins congeal and it dies.

Paulus Neef That's a good example. If you swim in your own sludge, you don't notice how it stinks—

or far too late. You need a distance from your own goings-on.

Ulrich Dietz Which is why you should always give insiders an outside eye.

Paulus Neef That applies to all industries. You have to repeatedly call yourself and your activities into question. That's where it starts.

Ulrich Dietz Apropos: What are your current goals?

Paulus Neef At the moment I'm trying to find out what's really essential to me and my family. What really moves and affects me. And because I can't stop myself I've recently founded MAMA, an ethical venture-capital corporation. We, a group of investors, managers, scientists and marketing specialists, want to support start-up entrepreneurs who are developing ideas and concepts in the area of sustainability. Next to education, social entrepreneurship and the Internet, sustainability is one of the great survival issues of our global society.

Ulrich Dietz Although the point is always to make money from all these wonderful utopias. Because social entrepreneurship only functions if the core business model of a company provides a steady foundation.

Paulus Neef Yes, and that's what I'm going to prove. I'm looking forward to it!

Susan Neiman

"The truth tells us how the world is. Morality tells us how it should be."

Susan Neiman

Rather than finish her high school degree,
Susan Neiman, who was born in Atlanta,
Georgia, in 1955, left school at fourteen
and lived for several years in communes in
Maryland and Berkeley. She began studying
philosophy at City College of New York, then
transferred to Harvard University and worked
as John Rawls's assistant. She went to Berlin
in 1982 on a Fulbright scholarship and spent
five years there, receiving her PhD in 1986
with a dissertation titled "The Unity of Reason
in Kant." Then she taught at Yale University
and Tel Aviv University. Since 2000, Neiman
has been director of the Einstein Forum in
Potsdam, where she lives with her son and
twin daughters. Her book *Evil in Modern
Thought* was translated into eight languages,
and her most recent publication, *Moral Clarity*,
will soon be published in German.

Albert Einstein was happiest in his summer house in Caputh, and probably one of his flashes of inspiration caused several cultural politicians to found the Einstein Forum in 1993 in its cheerful rooms. Now it is located in a renovated neoclassical building on the old market square in Potsdam, and like all the rooms there, the director's office is crowded and filled with books. That does not bother the striking professor much, after all, she deals with intellectual issues, and there are no limits on those. Like the man after which the institution is named, she radiates charm, can laugh resoundingly, and be charmingly funny. To insure she isn't hidden by her mountains of books in the portrait, we travel to another nucleus of the Enlightenment: the slightly less glamorous place where Frederick the Great liked to retreat to think: Sanssouci Palace.

Ulrich Dietz Your two most recent books, *Evil in Modern Thought* and *Moral Clarity,* gave me sleepless nights, but they were nevertheless informative.

Susan Neiman Why did you want to include me of all people in your book on the new new?

Ulrich Dietz Because you are a philosopher who has made enlightenment—the basic concept of Immanuel Kant's philosophy of reason—the focus of your studies. For me, enlightenment is a kind of primal substance of the advantages and disadvantages of Western modernism. On the one hand, it prepared the way for the new by eliminating certain privileges. On the other hand, it is probably in part responsible for the Western world's faith in technology. In the meanwhile we seem to believe that all our problems can be solved with the right technology. Yet that is a dubious ideology, as is demonstrated currently by the Western being haunted by fundamentalist terrorism and the associated image of the enemy. Overstating it somewhat, you could ask at this point: to what extent is the intellectual legacy of the Enlightenment in part responsible for the dominant ideologies: here Western totalitarian adoration of technology and there religious fanaticism?

Susan Neiman You're starting out *in medias res,* great. This set of themes is complex. Let me start out this way: at core, enlightenment is the faith that people can improve the world a little by their thoughts and actions.

Ulrich Dietz Does enlightenment have an innovative aspect? Is it visionary?

Susan Neiman It is, because it believes in ideals. It believes that ideals belong to reality; I emphasize: *belong to* it, not oppose it. Ideals are forms of reality that are better than the states in which we happen to be.

Ulrich Dietz Is that one of Kant's insights?

Susan Neiman Yes. The idealistic impulse wants to transcend that which is—be it our genetic bases or our environment. Remember the quotation on Kant's tombstone: *Two things fill the mind with ever new and increasing admiration and reverence, the more often and the more steadily one reflects on them: the starry heavens above me and the moral law within me.*
That is the balance between reason, which gives us morality, which reveals to us what people can do, and reverence, which reveals to us what we cannot do. We find ourselves between the two. What makes Kant highly charged even today is that because of this idealist impulse he insisted on a gulf, a difference between *Sein* and *Sollen,* between what is and what should be. This difference is, if you will, the birthplace of Kant's moral reason.

Ulrich Dietz And our problem is that we no longer make the distinction between what is and what should be?

Susan Neiman Exactly. The truth tells us how the world is. Morality tells us how it should be. It is a primal human need to question things as they are. Because we seek meaning.

Ulrich Dietz So that is the intersection between the moral and the ideal. In other words, a moral attitude is an idealistic attitude.

Susan Neiman Yes. Kant insisted that what is and what should be are of equal importance and value and that they should by no means be played off each other, as has been done constantly ever since. We are all born as part of nature, but we feel most alive when we transcend its limits. We do that often. Every time we explore the world rather than just be in it. Thus for me being human means rejecting the given as given.

Ulrich Dietz That means nothing other than that reality has to be measured by its ideals and not vice versa.

Susan Neiman Correct. All philosophers since Kant, with the exception of Hannah Arendt and Walter Benjamin, have tried to reduce what is to what should be. They wanted to eliminate this elementary difference. But we must live with the dualism of what is and what should be. We cannot eliminate this ambiguity; it is our nature.

Ulrich Dietz Is that not paradoxical?

Susan Neiman Yes. The essence of the ideal is that it cannot become reality. This paradox is part of the structure of our reason; it drives our constant search for meaning.

Ulrich Dietz You mean that one can only act morally if one is in a position to endure this paradox. And only then does one understand how necessary ideals are?

Susan Neiman Yes. My goal is that more people understand that Kantian idealism is an idealism for adults. It resists the wild utopianism of youth, but neither does it succumb to the cynicism of the disappointed ideals of youth. Our lifelong task is to reduce the gulf between what is and what should be in our own lives, always aware that it will never disappear entirely.

Ulrich Dietz Do you see Karl Popper as an heir to the Enlightenment?

Susan Neiman No, no, no! Popper is a positivist and hence someone who amputated the Enlightenment.

Positivism only acknowledges what can be proven scientifically, mathematically. It makes progress into an absolute and is thus ideological in the utmost. All other theories are at best tolerated—much like people who understand little about literature tolerate poetry. Just as Popper fixated solely on what is, Hegel and Marx concentrated just as one-sidedly on what should be. Karl Marx adopted the ideals of the Enlightenment, but he tried to integrate them into a materialistic basis in a radically reductionist way. For me, who started out as a Marxist, it was going too far that he understood every kind of ideal or religion as froth. For me, he abandoned the level of Enlightenment with that view.

Ulrich Dietz How do you really find something new in your field?

Susan Neiman In my field? Philosophy cannot be understood as a game. Unfortunately, some of my colleagues did just that. Not Theodor W. Adorno and Max Horkheimer, for example, but twentieth-century philosophy was dominated by linguistic analysis, and, with the exception of the great Ludwig Wittgenstein, it all revolved around whether this thing in front of me here is in fact a glass or whether I am just dreaming. Are phenomena real or not—but that's not how you get to the real questions! I only found those in the authors of the Enlightenment, who were centrally concerned with reality, suffering, and evil: in the work of Voltaire, Diderot, and above all Rousseau. Kant described him as the Newton of the mind—the highest compliment one could make of a colleague at the time.

Ulrich Dietz What revolutionary ideas made him the equal of Isaac Newton, who is considered one of the greatest scientists of all times?

Susan Neiman Rousseau was the first to treat the problem of evil philosophically, not theologically. He took the responsibility for evil away from God and gave it to human beings. And he considered evil a relative, a historical phenomenon, one that can be studied and thus made somewhat less evil. Just as evil came into the world, it can disappear from it again. Those were radically new ideas at the time.

Ulrich Dietz I had difficulties with an analogy about evil you made in your book. You compare the Lisbon earthquake, which destroyed that city in 1755 and killed thousands of its residents, with Auschwitz.

Susan Neiman Nearly everyone has difficulty with that. The background of it is that until the middle of the eighteenth century, the words "bad" and "evil" were equated, "malum". The Lisbon earthquake triggered a shock whose dimension was comparable to that of Auschwitz for the modern era.

Ulrich Dietz Probably every century has indeed had something like milestones of evil. One could ask why Auschwitz became synonymous with evil and not, say, the Chinese Cultural Revolution or the Stalinist purges.

Susan Neiman Both the events you mention could indeed be considered even more evil, if one concentrates on the fact that they killed not only—in quotation marks—people but also ideals. What was the goal of Auschwitz? To kill certain groups of people because they were considered unworthy of life.

Ulrich Dietz I find all three mentalities are equally sick and inhuman.

Susan Neiman Inhuman, yes. But they are not equally sick but rather sick in different ways. Not because typhus, say, would be worse than malaria. If one argues morally as I do, the specific forms of evil have to be analyzed precisely. My aim is to undemonize the concept of evil. So that we can think with it again.

Ulrich Dietz If you look at what the Bush government did, it's easy to lose faith in a lot of good. Faced with American imperialism, one can even ask who caused 9/11.

Susan Neiman You are referring to the conspiracy theories that suggest the CIA was responsible for the destruction of the Twin Towers? We will never be able to prove that one way or the other. What is documented, however, is that at the time Bush loudly expressed his joy with the words: "Lucky me! I hit the trifecta!" According to the White House transcript, he uttered the phrase thirteen times!

Ulrich Dietz You see what an unprecedented benefit this catastrophe was for defense industry.

Susan Neiman Bush, Cheney, Rumsfeld, and Rice committed evil. You have to call a spade a spade.

Ulrich Dietz You were committed in your support for Barack Obama.

Susan Neiman Absolutely. We were standing at the abyss. It was our historic opportunity—and it still is.

Ulrich Dietz In your publications, you dared to cross boundaries. That requires a certain courage, and that brings us back to Kant and his statement: "Have the courage to use your own understanding!"

Susan Neiman That's it exactly! Kant is always simple and always profound.

Ulrich Dietz Do you feel courageous?

Susan Neiman More like angry. Perhaps my fury makes me courageous. I wanted to write a book that would also address the fundamentalists of the Midwest and their repulsive double standard.

Ulrich Dietz The title of your new book, *Moral Clarity*, refers to a Bush phrase.

Susan Neiman As a philosopher, I wanted to reclaim this idiom, which he stole, and present it in his immorality.

Ulrich Dietz You mean Bush's "axis of evil"?

Susan Neiman Exactly. The Republicans occupied the territory of morality, and I wanted to take it back from these right-wing reactionaries. Because the liberal camp had, regrettably, completely negated it, almost discriminated against it. Words such as "hero," "noble," and "ideal" sounded suspicious in liberal ears and for a long time were even taboo—a huge mistake.

Ulrich Dietz Fascination with the topos of the hero is undiminished, albeit decidedly controversial.

Susan Neiman Right. In the summer of 2009, I invited people to a conference at the Einstein Forum that I titled *Heroism Reconsidered*. The reaction was overwhelmingly positive.

Ulrich Dietz How did you, as an American philosopher, end up at the Einstein Forum Potsdam?

Susan Neiman Let me tell you a little bit about the Forum first. It was founded in 1993 as an interdisciplinary platform for scholarship in the former private home of Albert Einstein: his summer home, where he, as he said, spent the happiest time of his life. Shortly after the fall of the Berlin Wall, the Land of Brandenburg wanted to set an example and establish a link to Potsdam's traditional role as a center of the Enlightenment since Frederick the Great. Presumably I was chosen because I had been doing research in and publishing on this field for some time. And because I had already been teaching both in Tel Aviv and in Yale. For me, heading the Forum is a dream job, because I am no longer in an ivory tower as I once was but can instead get involved in debates about society.

Ulrich Dietz Have we become more moral?

Susan Neiman We have certainly made moral progress. For example, I grew up in Georgia. My mother was involved in the Civil Rights Movement early on. It is truly burned into my memory that we were not allowed to attend the same schools as black children and not allowed to swim with them in the lake. At that time—which was, after all, the 1960s—it was inconceivable that less than fifty years later we would have a black, female secretary of state!

Ulrich Dietz To say nothing of a black president.

Susan Neiman Exactly. The second example is that we women have also achieved a great deal within two generations. We can see that from how self-determinedly our daughters grow up when compared to us. The third example is torture. Even just three hundred years ago, people paid admission to witness the most brutal public executions.

Ulrich Dietz But unfortunately today the Internet is a virtual place where millions of people obviously very often watch as others are subjected to suffering.

Susan Neiman I am well aware of that, and also that torture was legalized again under Bush. But progress is not linear.

Ulrich Dietz At nineteen, you went from Atlanta to Harvard, where you studied with such luminaries as John Rawls and Stanley Cavell. Yet you never received a high school diploma and left school at fourteen. Where you a wunderkind or a radical?

Susan Neiman More like a crossover artist. Another aspect of my biography is my three children, a boy and twin girls, whom I raised as a single mother. The one thing does not preclude the other—on the contrary, they can represent an enrichment.

Ulrich Dietz What can we learn from this: let women raise children and succeed in their careers. That too will lead to new things. The antithesis is fundamentalist societies that repress women, as we see again and again.

Susan Neiman It's true: anyone who believes the Enlightenment is outdated should look at Afghanistan.

Ulrich Dietz The irony of history is that Kant's categorical imperative—"act in accordance with a maxim of ends that it can be a universal law for everyone to have"—would do our still recession-plagued times a lot of good; it would be more present. What remains to us of the Enlightenment?

Susan Neiman There are four values I have tried to liberate from the clichés that are wrongly associated with the Enlightenment: happiness, reason, reverence, and hope. The new aspect of the idea of happiness is the universally guaranteed right of happiness, as expressed in the American Declaration of Independence as the "pursuit of happiness." Happiness as the new goal of human beings on earth was truly a revolutionary ideal—revolutionary not because the advocates of the Enlightenment were stupid and did not see evil but precisely because they saw it! Since the Enlightenment, we no longer consider an earthquake like the terrible one in Haiti in January 2010 punishment by God or the work of the devil but rather a natural catastrophe. Happiness is an active value.

Ulrich Dietz And reason?

Susan Neiman Likewise. The declaration of faith in reason is by no means opposed to emotions and passion but it prevents superstition and blind obedience to authority. I mean reason as a source of ideals, a reason of education, which wants and strives for something better than that which is.

Ulrich Dietz Reason is the key to the ideal?

Susan Neiman Exactly. It is, in any case, not about some mathematical formulas. The third value is reverence, in contrast to piety. The Enlightenment took a stand against orthodox religion but it was by no means atheistic. Reverence meant respect for creation itself, independently of a potential creator. This basic moral idea is more relevant than ever before, because we are intently aware that our globe, the Earth, which feeds us and keeps us alive, is more at risk than ever. In addition, reverence calls for a sense of gratitude, which in turn makes generosity possible. Generosity has to be cultivated in order to be grateful. Finally: hope. It is not about blind faith in progress, not about the naïve idea that people are all good. Hope is the driving force for other values, the conviction that we can change the world.

Lisa Randall

"The world is more than that which we see."

Lisa Randall

Her book *Warped Passages* made this expert on
particle physics, string theory, and cosmology,
who was born in New York in 1962, the new
star of a generation of scientists who are trying
to convey highly complex information to a
popular audience. The mathematical talent
of the second of three daughters of a salesman
and a teacher was already evident in school.
In 1987 Lisa Randall received her dissertation at Harvard, became an assistant professor
and later associate professor at Massachusetts
Institute of Technology, and in 1998 she was
the first woman to be appointed to a chair for
theoretical physics at Princeton. Since 2001
Randall has been teaching at Harvard. She
loves to cross boundaries of every kind.
Recently she wrote the libretto for an opera
by the Spanish composer Hèctor Parra and
is currently working on a book on the secrets
of the universe.

Once we have made our way through the labyrinth of rooms at Harvard to her wing, her assistant explains to us that the professor will be late, but we should go ahead and take a seat in her office. It is not easy to find a free chair, because the physicist's office is overflowing with masses of paper. The wall-sized green board, scribbled full with columns of numbers and equations, is the only calm spot between the piles of journals and files. A little later, Lisa Randall storms in, in a splendid mood, because the opera she collaborated on had its premiere the previous evening—a great success! She quickly clears the sofa and a chair, sits facing us, and asks us to start, as her next appointment is already waiting. The speed with which she speaks is phenomenal, dictated by the tempo of her thinking. As a scientist, she moves in spheres with which few are familiar, but more and more she is discovering her artistic side. Perhaps one day she will begin to compose? She smiles and remains inscrutably silent.

Ulrich Dietz As a theoretical physicist, specializing in particle physics, string theory, and cosmology, you explore unknown, additional dimensions of the universe beyond our four-dimensional space-time world. You describe these "hidden dimensions" of the universe in your book in such an exciting way that this complex theme becomes very clear even to people like me with a limited understanding of physics.

Lisa Randall Thank you. I wanted to write a basic book about the nature of matter and space-time, of the forces of the universe and of what happens in it. I worked on many subjects in particle physics and didn't enter directly into the study of extra dimensions. Before taking this subject seriously, I was working on supersymmetry, a speculated theory that presumes that for every particle we know, there is an additional one. This theory has effects on the standard model of particle physics: a theory, now thirty years old, about the essence of matter and the forces that interact with one another thanks to their elementary components. Yet our standard model cannot answer some fundamental questions. Supersymmetry might address some of these, but has problems of its own when confronting the data we have acquired about elementary particles and their interactions. When searching for solutions to these mysteries, my collaborator Raman Sundrum and I entered extradimensional worlds.

Ulrich Dietz It is difficult to imagine a five-dimensional model of the universe. What might it look like?

Lisa Randall It is indeed almost impossible to visualize, because we are accustomed to thinking and operating in the three categories of space and the dimension of time. But the world is more than that which we see. Why shouldn't there be other dimensions? Simply because we don't see them? No. They can either be so tiny or so curved that they are hidden from our perception, even if infinite in size.

Ulrich Dietz Can you explain that in a little more detail?

Lisa Randall The key question is not whether these extra dimensions exist, but rather what do we know about them? Raman Sundrum and I started with Albert Einstein's theory of relativity, which says that space and time are integrated into a space-time fabric, which is deformed, curved, and distorted by mass and energy. In 1999 we discovered that an invisible extra dimension can stretch out to infinity, provided it is suitably distorted in a curved space-

time. An extra dimension can be infinite in size – but nonetheless hidden.

Ulrich Dietz In contrast to most other scientists, you make no exact measurements and calculations. Instead, you speculate and begin to leave out unknown parameters, much like is done in mathematics, in order to make it possible to solve equations. In the process you run into new possibilities, and perhaps gain access to new dimensions in this way.

Lisa Randall Our ideas are indeed speculative, but they are motivated by interesting theoretical thoughts. Some of the most challenging theories address the question of why gravity is so much weaker than the other forces and those give rise to testable fingerprints.

Ulrich Dietz Haven't we known since Isaac Newton why gravity keeps us on the ground with both legs?

Lisa Randall Gravitation only seems powerful to us because the earth has so much mass. But even so a tiny magnet can pick up a paperclip even though the total mass of the Earth is pulling in the opposite direction. So why is gravitation so powerless against the attraction of a small magnet? One possibility is that gravity exists in a fifth dimension that distorts it so much that gravity in our location in the fifth dimension seems weak. To explain this in detail, I would have to tell you something about string theory and the role of branes.

Ulrich Dietz Go for it.

Lisa Randall According to string theory, the basic units in nature are not pointlike particles but oscillating strings, which themselves presume more than three spatial dimensions. If string theory correctly describes the universe, then it could also contain higher-dimensional objects known as branes. A brane is a membrane-like, low-dimensional object, located like an island in a higher-dimensional space, and it can contain energy and enclose particles and forces.

Ulrich Dietz I'm all ears.

Lisa Randall In the model we developed, the universe consists of two branes: the Gravitybrane and the Weakbrane, each of which borders a finitely large fifth dimension. This fifth dimension is very warped. We are sitting on the Weakbrane, to which all forces and materials are linked. Gravity is concentrated near the Gravitybrane, where it is essentially as powerful as the other forces. But because space is so extremely warped, gravity is much weaker at the Weakbrane, where we reside.

Ulrich Dietz Can the particle accelerator at CERN (Conseil Européen pour la Recherche Nucléaire, or European Organization for Nuclear Research) in Geneva prove this fifth dimension exists?

Lisa Randall Exactly. My colleagues there are working on empirical proofs.

Ulrich Dietz In Europe, CERN is considered a mecca of experimental physics.

Lisa Randall Yes. For us physicists, March 30, 2010, was a historic day. For the first time, colleagues at the LHC particle accelerator, the Large Hadron Collider, a subterranean ring twenty-seven kilometers in diameter, caused proton rays moving in the opposite direction near the speed of light to collide. The hope is to create high energies like those that existed billions of seconds after the big bang 13.7 billion years ago.

Ulrich Dietz How do these particle collisions reveal hints of our extra dimensions?

Lisa Randall If the fifth dimension does indeed exist, we would hope to discover previously unknown particles that can move through the extra dimension that would appear to us as heavy new particles.

Ulrich Dietz And if such particles are not found?

Lisa Randall Let's wait five to ten years. And if my theories turn out to be wrong, we'll move on. Science too is always about trial and error.

Ulrich Dietz Researchers have to be patient people. Often years pass between the idea and its proof.

Lisa Randall And sometimes decades. Consider the Higgs particle. The physicist Peter Higgs of the University of Edinburgh predicted it more than forty years before it was discovered. Here too we are placing our hopes on the CERN's new particle accelerator. We scientists cannot produce detailed timetables that we work through. Now and again, rarely, chance unexpectedly provides us suddenly with knowledge. Our journey has just begun.

Ulrich Dietz What projects are you working on now?

Lisa Randall I have been thinking a great deal about dark matter, of what it is composed and how it could be visualized. After all, it makes up the majority of the material of the cosmos. And I am writing a new book.

Ulrich Dietz What will it be about?

Lisa Randall The book will probably be titled *Knocking on Heaven's Door*. It's about the physics going on today like that at the LHC. But it's also about what science is, how it develops, and how the exotic ex-perimental consequences physicists now study indeed tell us the truth about the universe. The book is perhaps broader than my first, which I like since it's more interesting than repeating myself, and gives me new opportunities to think about big questions.

Ulrich Dietz Do your excursions into other areas inspire you to discoveries in your specialty?

Lisa Randall That would be nice, but it's not the case. When I write or dedicate myself to other projects, like the opera *Hypermusic Prologue* recently, I find it broadens my world. I also think such projects do lead to new creations. The young Spanish composer Hèctor Parra was very much inspired by science as was the American installation artist who did the sets, Matthew Ritchie.

Ulrich Dietz You worked on an opera?

Lisa Randall Yes. Hèctor proposed that I write a libretto based on my theories of extra dimensions and multiverses. I did it, and it was a fantastic experience. This cross-over of art and science is rather fashionable in general at the moment; in Hèctor's case, however, it was even more natural, since he is the son of a physicist. It was a wonderful experience for me to be able to work together with such ideal partners as Matthew Ritchie. He designed an intriguing stage set composed of ornamental lattice structures, and swirling video projections imbued with psychedelic colors.

Ulrich Dietz Was the idea to illustrate your mysterious unknown dimensions?

Lisa Randall Yes, but in the end it might have been easier to follow if it was a bit more literal. I did abstract physics, Hèctor did abstract music, and Matthew did abstract art. Perhaps something to pin down that people readily understood would have been useful. Nonetheless the project was an exciting metaphor for the imagination. Not just in physics but really in all fields, more and more people are trying to change their perspective. Musicians, artists, and physicists all want to invent or discover something new. The feeling I wanted to convey is that creative people feel that something is missing, that there is much more than what we have known hitherto.

Ulrich Dietz That's right. This creative unrest is the impulse and the driving force to change direction, to move around in foreign realms, to cross boundaries, or, like you, to speculate on theory. Now that you are so famous well beyond the world of physics, what is your biggest challenge?

Lisa Randall I don't know about that. But I love the challenges of entering new arenas. I enjoyed thinking about how to transform abstract ideas into language, sound, or images, but of course I enjoy the physics, too, especially with the LHC now working at long last.

Ulrich Dietz Your talent for physics and mathematics is a great gift.

Lisa Randall At school I liked mathematics because all the tasks had clear and intelligible solutions. Though what I now work on is abstract, ironically perhaps I studied physics because it is not quite so abstract and has a connection to the real world.

Ulrich Dietz Were there always scientists in your family?

Lisa Randall No. My mother was an elementary school teacher, and my father did study engineering, but was more involved in sales. I was the first to become a professor and my younger sister soon followed. She teaches computer science.

Ulrich Dietz In the mid-1980s, after university, I had an opportunity to work for a mechanical engineering firm that was experimenting with laser technology. That was still terra incognita in Germany at the time. We were working on possibilities, then still quite unfamiliar, of splitting metal with laser beams. In addition to theory, it was essentially about practical value. That is, about how this technology could be employed. Do you sometimes miss not having more concrete results in your work?

Lisa Randall I enjoy pure theory, but I agree it's great when you can connect to the world with some ap-plications. Perhaps this is part of the reason why I wrote a book and did this opera.

Ulrich Dietz Perhaps you need a certain rigor of discipline as a precondition to be able to deviate in a focused way. We are speaking of the age-old phenomenon of chaos and order, each of which conditions the other. Especially when developing technologically ambitious products, we experience this often. As a researcher, haven't you ever thought, now and again, of going into industry, in part because you would make more money there?

Lisa Randall Not really. I wanted the creative freedom you get in a university setting. People outside academia are excited too about these ideas, as I've seen with the great response I'm still getting to my book. People who have probably never thought about the universe before, much less multiverses, are reading it and sending me enthusiastic letters!

Ulrich Dietz You wrote it when you were confined to bed for some time after a rock-climbing accident?

Lisa Randall Yes, I broke my heel and had to spend two months lying down. But it took three years to finish my book.

Ulrich Dietz You begin every chapter with verses from pop songs. Right at the beginning there are two lines from Fleetwood Mac: "You can go your own way. Go your own way." Is that your motto?

Lisa Randall No, I don't have a motto or higher authorities. I simply try to make a contribution to getting the cosmos to reveal its secrets one day.

René Redzepi

"The new luxury is a carrot!"

René Redzepi

Of all people, a Dane has occupied the number one spot on the list of the world's greatest chefs since mid-2010, the youngest yet to reach that spot. René Redzepi, born in Copenhagen in 1977, the son of a Danish mother and an Albanian-Macedonian father, has won over the global community of gourmets with his gastronomy of first-class ingredients entirely from Nordic sources. At his restaurant, Noma, the student of the Catalan star of molecular cuisine, Ferran Adrià, composes in the rhythm of the seasons, using moss and musk ox, reindeer and herbs, king crabs and cloudberries in unbelievably delicate ways. Now Scandinavian cuisine once again tastes as unforgettable as the landscape: like tangy, aromatic seawater and wild fjords.

Noma is located in a former warehouse in Christianshavn, a picturesque district of Copenhagen. It is nine in the morning when we enter the double glass doors. But the chef and his young coworkers have already been standing for two hours at tables in the back of the restaurant in their white coats and dark aprons. They are unpacking groceries, washing, cutting, chopping herbs and vegetables, and sorting and pureeing fruit—the boss right alongside them. The elongated room with ceiling-high windows, brightly stained plank floors, and exposed-beam ceiling was designed by Redzepi and the Copenhagen-based architect Signe Bindslev Henriksen. It was his idea to hang reindeer pelts over the leather-upholstered armchairs around solid oak tables: Scandinavian purism with an extravagant accent. For Redzepi has an eccentric touch, which is also expressed in his cuisine. Who else composes dishes according to color or serves wild boar tartare made from ingredients that the boar eats?

Ulrich Dietz When did you start your day today?

René Redzepi As always, at 6 a.m. When I work, I sleep three to four hours on average. Our nights often end at 2:30 in the morning, sometimes, when we have events, not until 3:30. There's a lot of time pressure. We work a lot and sleep too little, and despite our success the finances remain uncertain.

Ulrich Dietz That is a problem for a lot of people with creative work. How old is your restaurant, Noma?

René Redzepi Six years. We opened in November 2003.

Ulrich Dietz It's a beautiful space, reduced to the essentials! Who designed it?

René Redzepi The interior designer and architect Signe Henriksen designed it with our input, of course. I wanted a transparent ambience, one that countered the clichés of gourmet restaurants. No palatial splendor, no glittering fabrics, no heavy silverware, no giant plates of delicate porcelain on which orange splashes of pumpkin soup float. All this to me seems quite artificial, very far from where it comes from and what it originally was. It no longer feels real. So many people have obviously lost any sense of roots. They sit in superficial restaurants…

Ulrich Dietz …which are only about the façade, is that what you mean?

René Redzepi Yes. They no longer appreciate the genuine, the unadulterated, the craft. Look at this table of heavy oak at which we are sitting. It is a table, no more and no less.

Ulrich Dietz The best of its kind. Isn't that the charm of the Scandinavian aesthetic, the feeling for the simple and clear?

René Redzepi Yes, functional, to the point, transparent. It's true, our design tradition is in demand again. The bling era is coming to an end. The new luxury is a carrot! No longer rare types of fish, or caviar. The new luxury is the perfect carrot, grown by the best farmers in the best soil with the best seed, cooked in the perfect stock, and cooked by passionate people. It is becoming more and more difficult to find people with this attitude today.

Ulrich Dietz That is presumably the reason for your great success, even internationally now. You are booked months in advance.

René Redzepi We don't prepare the fish any better than anyone else, but perhaps our motivation is different.

Ulrich Dietz For me, what you do is avant-garde. It is not the molecular gastronomy of Ferran Adrià, with whom you also studied, it's a new, innovative cuisine with no high-tech extravagance or exalted surprises. How did it come about?

René Redzepi My father is from Macedonia, my mother from Denmark. I was born in Copenhagen but till the war broke out I grew up partly in Tetovo near Skopje. The different mentalities of my parents certainly influenced me. Perhaps it made it easier for me to discover my own basic idea. It is simple: we concentrate on regional products. Our guests are meant to rediscover where they are in the world and what season it is. Time and place. In many restaurants today, when you close your eyes and taste, you can no longer tell where you are, whether it's Paris, São Paulo, or Stuttgart, your native city.

Ulrich Dietz Why have we lost our sense of our roots?

René Redzepi I'm not a macho, and I haven't studied the history of food, but I think it might have disappeared gradually, ever since fewer and fewer women cook regularly for their families. Instead, we look more and more to prepared foods and junk food and then on the other end of the scale capricious, expensive ingredients from exotic regions.

Ulrich Dietz But there are more cookbooks on the market than ever before, more food shows, more fancy restaurants.

René Redzepi That's show, a masquerade! Hiding behind that are people who no longer make the effort to cook themselves. One clear proof of that is how little money people on average are willing to spend for high-quality food—much less than they spend on clothing, for example. For most people, the façade matters more than the substance.

Ulrich Dietz So you think we have lost our sense of the genuine?

René Redzepi In Scandinavia, as in most Northern European countries, people scorn their tradition as farmers. In the meantime, we have one food scandal after another here; the supermarkets keep tons of rotten meat. People no longer even know what bad food is. They can no longer taste because of all the flavor enhancers.

Ulrich Dietz Is that primarily true of Western society?

René Redzepi I think so. In my opinion, Japan is a wonderful counterexample. Chefs there experiment month after month with subtle culinary changes. Celebrating their cuisine is part of their tradition. At the same time, they welcome other schools and integrate them.

Ulrich Dietz That's your approach as well. What is your cuisine based on?

René Redzepi In essence, it consists of what I like to eat myself. We have never put together a menu to satisfy any projected tastes of our guests. So there is fish, shellfish for example, and above all vegetables. Vegetables are incredibly diverse and have so many nuances of tastes. They have so many different states in which they can be used, and they always feel light: seeds, fruit, plants, flowers, greens. They can contain lots of protein. For example, we also serve a menu of fresh vegetable juices in lieu of wine. I also consider it healthy to have a menu that changes with the rhythm of the seasons. We have to find our inner hunter-gatherer again, when we eat. And we have to learn to cook more simply with better products. In fact, there shouldn't be any bad restaurants in the world, because there are so many terrific products!

Ulrich Dietz That sounds great, especially because it enables you to change the way you live fundamentally with little effort. I find it fascinating that you, with your radical approach, were selected the best chef in the world and were awarded two stars. On the other hand, isn't the pressure on you enormous?

René Redzepi Oh yes, and on top of that, we are a restaurant that always tries to move forward. We cannot and do not want to allow ourselves to stand still, to repeat ourselves. And under no circumstances do I ever want to switch on the autopilot. So we have to evolve and constantly develop our cuisine. Many of our guests fly in once a month; they want to try something new.

Ulrich Dietz How and above all when do you invent your creations? For example, Ferran Adrià returns to his laboratory in Barcelona for six months of every year. What have you learned from him?

René Redzepi To be free. It was the sense of freedom he conveyed to me. For me, cooking is a craft. I don't necessarily see myself as an artist who creates for the sake of art but rather as a service provider. My creativity is a talent for living with nature. Everything else results from that.

Ulrich Dietz So you and your team are constantly improving.

René Redzepi Everything on the menu is what our fishermen, hunters, and farmers recommend.

Ulrich Dietz The ingredients are one thing, but what you make from them is a new cuisine, a new gourmet style. How does that succeed?

René Redzepi You mean, what inspires me? Very different things and aspects: an old style for preparing something, say, or often colors. Once we composed a menu of bright red colors. It was February, and we had fresh langoustines, and when we cooked them, they turned carmine red. We arranged herbs and vegetables and flowers in similar colors around them. Not only did it look like everything belonged together, but it also tested incredible! We do the same with white and yellow, white blueberries, say, pine shoots, or heather, or with saddle of venison, which we serve with snails and wild sprouts of the forest—with all the things the animal steps on when it goes through the forest and with the things it eats. Or we make wild boar tartare, but not from boar meat but from the things boars eat. Or I bite into a carrot that has a kind of spiciness and seems to taste like some other spice. Then I find that spice and combine it with the carrot.

Ulrich Dietz Terrific examples! So your approach is more intuitive?

René Redzepi Often. But we work for weeks on certain ideas. Like how to break the code of cabbage. It is very difficult. Cabbage remains cabbage, but I want it full of aroma, light and juicy. We experimented for a long time and now we have succeeded. It's true, intuition is crucial for me. I don't want to create fashions that I present in turn from season to season like a collection of clothes. Imagine the weather changes tomorrow and it's below freezing and the wind is whistling.

Ulrich Dietz Then you change your menu overnight?

René Redzepi More or less. After one night of frost, the lettuces are frozen, so we have to react quickly. Even then our slogan is back to time and place.

Ulrich Dietz Are you, like most pioneers, a perfectionist?

René Redzepi Unfortunately, our material rules out perfectionism, because it is unpredictable. For me, perfection exists only in the sense of approaching an imagined ideal for my cooking.

Ulrich Dietz How often do you change your menu?

René Redzepi Constantly, sometimes eight times a month. The components change several times a week.

Ulrich Dietz Let's talk about balancing creativity and money. Nearly all the star chefs finance their restaurants not through their guests but through additional marketing activities. They publish books, appear on cooking shows, sell sauces, and so on. Do you consider that the right path, or shouldn't the menus and food be much more expensive?

René Redzepi A difficult question. Star chefs dedicate themselves more or less full-time to marketing their label. They make appearances, and let other people make up the recipes. It's a shame that people talk about the art of cooking but there are no cultural subsidies available for it. I don't have a car, and I live with my wife and daughter in a small rented apartment. To earn a reasonable amount, I would have to double our prices, as in some restaurants in Paris, where a set menu costs 345 euros and maybe they are not even making money.

Ulrich Dietz You would have to educate people that they need to pay more for top quality. The problem is the same everywhere: it is difficult to make a profit with creativity because there are no objective criteria.

René Redzepi It's true. I think there are very, very few restaurants that could get away with such prices. In art, perhaps it's easier, then collectors or clients say: "I don't like it, but I can see that it's good." With cooking, by contrast, you hear without exception: "I don't like it, so it's bad." Food is very, very subjective.

Ulrich Dietz Frequently people go to gourmet restaurants that are in. They respect neither the outstanding work of the chefs nor the excellent ingredients. Because they never learned to do so. Really, we have to teach our children respect for food beginning in pre-school and teach them in a playful way how to cook.

René Redzepi Yes. In general, people are not aware that good products are healthier.

Ulrich Dietz Isn't it sometimes difficult to limit your products to the immediate region?

René Redzepi On the contrary. I've learned that this self-imposed limitation makes me more inventive.

Ulrich Dietz The most difficult thing is maintaining your own standard. What do you find most frustrating about your profession?

René Redzepi When I have the feeling I am standing still, when nothing occurs to me. There are phases like that. Thank God, they don't last. And sometimes I'm just tired. As a chef today, you are under extreme pressure, especially from the omnipresence of the media. You have to serve them, give interviews, travel to conferences. You have no choice if you don't want to lose the attention of the public on which your existence and that of your coworkers depends. At the same time, you have to be in the kitchen—sometimes it's a real test of endurance.

Ulrich Dietz I understand all too well. I work in the IT business, a fast-moving industry where new technologies are invented in short cycles. Moreover, we are listed on the stock-exchange, so every quarter I have to tell the public where we stand. If possible, the results should always be better. At first, I felt a lot of pressure, but in the meantime I'm pretty relaxed. Especially in our hyper-accelerated world, we have to ask ourselves what is important to us. You have developed a new Nordic gourmet gastronomy, in which the innovation lies precisely in taking a step backward. Not searching for the thing that could be the next, even more refined kick after molecular gastronomy. I find that terrific. The important thing is to understand what really adds quality to life. To form and shape something new, you don't always have to be more dynamic and faster but, on the contrary, slower. Bring down the tempo in order to move forward.

René Redzepi I agree with you absolutely—in theory! In practice, however, we have reached the limit of our capacities.

Ulrich Dietz Do you then have to accept more media opportunities, or open more restaurants?

René Redzepi I have a lot of such offers. Thus far, though, nothing has been interesting enough, because I believe that my work will get worse. Perhaps it will be worn out and watered down. I never wanted to be a big brand, never wanted to work just for profit but rather for its own sake. I would never allow this restaurant to become a money machine. The day I notice I am switching on the autopilot, I will leave and do something else. I don't want to become a parody of myself.

Ulrich Dietz That is a crucial point. I have often talked to people who want to expand and explained to them the problems they face: even more stress, even less time, no more private life. The price is extremely high. What drives you to constantly dare to do new things?

René Redzepi Primarily impatience. And boredom. I get bored easily. When I have achieved something, I begin to get bored. But I haven't gotten there yet. I am still working on seeing how far I can go with this cuisine. How important my country can become in gastronomy.

Ulrich Dietz Do you believe Nordic cuisine will lead the way in the future?

René Redzepi Only if we soon have more restaurants in our category.

Ulrich Dietz Did you always want to be a chef?

René Redzepi Yes. I have realized my dream. I'm very happy, actually.

John&
Paul&
Ringo&
George.

"It's about shifting perspectives and breaking the mold."

Tobias Rehberger

Because one can never be certain that things are what they seem to be, Tobias Rehberger, born in Esslingen in 1966, has for twenty-five years been rigorously shifting the perspectives with which people define reality. In 1995, this unconventional thinker, who studied with Martin Kippenberger and Thomas Bayrle, asked fellow artists to tell him their favorite flowers and then portrayed them as vases. Since then the now world-famous sculptor, currently prorector at the Städelschule in Frankfurt, whirls together perception patterns in such a liberating way with his often neon-colored, usually functional objects and installations that both cognitive and physical pleasure are guaranteed. In 2009 he received the Golden Lion at the fifty-third Venice Biennale for his environments at the intersection of sculpture and design. For art is in the eye of the beholder.

His studio is located in a rear courtyard in Frankfurt's Mitte district; it occupies two floors, and depending on the project there are sometimes as many as two or three dozen assistants. There are more than enough exhibitions and commissions, as Tobias Rehberger is in demand internationally as a sculptor; he also designs cafés, gardens, and soon even a bridge. On this morning, however, it's rather calm; an assistant opens the door, and the artist appears right behind her in a white T-shirt. "Let's go to the conference room," he says, "we'll have the most room there." The tables are pushed together to form a square; the walls are white and empty—it is a place for thinking and planning, not tinkering as in the workshop downstairs. A few objects are standing in the latter, being modeled, assembled, painted, waxed, or coated with plastic by assistants. Rehberger himself gets involved, if at all, only at the end; he is the director. "Does it bother you if I smoke," he asks. Not at all, a good idea, with black coffee you can even permit yourself a cigar. You need a touch of bohemia.

Ulrich Dietz Tobias, you describe yourself as a sculptor. What fascinates me most is how you walk the line between art and design. Your works are both sculptures in the classical sense and everyday objects that need to be used: chairs, tables, lamps, screens, vases. Recently you've been designing increasingly larger urban projects—cafés, a bridge. But they're always at the intersection of art and design. They're hybrid. What interests you in this?

Tobias Rehberger The hybrid interests me as an aesthetic that exemplifies how there are multiple perspectives to everything, depending on your chosen standpoint. As soon as you alter the context or the terms of reference, the objects are transformed. They turn into something else. Why shouldn't a sculpture also be a comfortable seat? Breaking open the mental prisons we're all stuck inside—that's what my work is about.

Ulrich Dietz Are artists prototypes for innovation?

Tobias Rehberger That's a question about the definition of art. My key question is always: What perspective do I approach something with? What is my view of it? Art is what I see as art. It doesn't exist in and of itself, no matter whether it's a unique piece or a ready-made. You can, in principle, saw a hammer into little pieces and eat it. But a hammer is more successful if you use it to put nails in the wall. In the same way I can analyze a chair from the perspective of ergonomic seating or the history of design, or of course art.

Ulrich Dietz So for you the ability to observe phenomena, things and people from continually new and different perspectives is innovative?

Tobias Rehberger Yes. Or at least it's central to my work, which comes from a basic mistrust. I think that if you want to do something new, you need a problem. My problem, if you like, is this deeply rooted scepticism. With everything I look at or deal with I ask myself whether it could function differently. Is it right what they say about the meaning and being of this thing? Or are there quite different ways of understanding it, literally and in a metaphorical sense. Is it perhaps more successful and more complex in other circumstances, in a different context?

Ulrich Dietz The example of the hammer and nail…

Tobias Rehberger Precisely. I can't really believe myself how I piece the world together.

Ulrich Dietz Which is why you call it into question and can go in a new direction. Remarkable. In the beginning there's a handicap. Isn't this comparable to Demosthenes, who overcame his stammer to become the greatest orator of his time?

Tobias Rehberger I think there are two principle possibilities for pushing forward to something new. Either by having a problem, or from a playful, detached process of trying things out. Even though I don't really have a problem with this glass in front of me, I can think about what it might be good for apart from being filled with liquid. You can experiment with something in all directions, naively and without aim or intention. Sometimes this brings about something new and refreshing.

Ulrich Dietz Is your art a kind of derivation of what you might do differently in the world, a materialization of your ideas?

Tobias Rehberger You could put it like that. Although I've chosen the field of art because it's where I can present my subject matter in the most exemplary way. You can be creative in any career. Whether baker or banker is not the point.

Ulrich Dietz So what is?

Tobias Rehberger That someone feels something to be a problem that isn't one for other people. That's the real point!

Ulrich Dietz Do you mean that the trigger is a lack, or an emergency situation?

Tobias Rehberger Or simply having fun with finding problems! That can be very satisfying. You don't do art to become rich or save lives.

Ulrich Dietz What's the fun in a work like the *Tea Ceremony?*

Tobias Rehberger OK, I was quite involved at the time with the traditional Japanese aesthetic and its perfectionism. There's a claim to truth in its rigid rituals—and, as you now know, I have a problem with that. With this assertion that there's only one beatific form or activity.

Ulrich Dietz Were you annoyed by the element of total control?

Tobias Rehberger That too. Because it so essentially contradicts my character.

Ulrich Dietz And how is it with *Tsutsumu,* a snow-covered bench in a Japanese garden?

Tobias Rehberger That work has a similar reference. There's this accurate little garden, and the snow that falls on it every morning turns it into an amorphous entity. When it's completely covered with snow, it loses all contour; it's deformed into a light dumpling.

This clash, the collision of order and chaos, is what fascinates me. The paradoxical dependency of the one on the other. In the morning, before the sun rises, there's this pile, and then the snow melts to reveal the perfect constructiveness and symmetry.

Ulrich Dietz Does art need iconoclasm?

Tobias Rehberger Hm. I always tell my students: learn to be honest with yourselves, ask what's bothering you. And start from there! Without problems there isn't any really good art, because you always remain attached to the status quo. If you imagine this as chewing gum, you have to do something with it that alters it. But it can't lose too much shape—to stay with the image—because there always needs to be the possibility of feedback. Only then is art innovative, when it extends the status quo.

Ulrich Dietz When it breaks the mold?

Tobias Rehberger However you like to put it. Disturb the conditions within which you're operating, but don't get disturbed yourself. Vincent van Gogh was driven to the edge of madness by this, but only to the edge.

Ulrich Dietz He didn't completely call into question the system of art that gave him a sense of identity…

Tobias Rehberger Right. You can't yourself leave the space that defines you. Sometimes students bring me works that are consistently thought through and made, but that lack the element of otherness, perhaps only a minimal difference, that distinguishes good art from great art. You shouldn't want to make good art, but simply ART.

Ulrich Dietz And the market aspect? How far can the market be manipulated—by gallerists, curators or auctioneers, for example? Hasn't there recently been a considerable amount of market-savvy—and for this reason hyped—modish art?

Tobias Rehberger That doesn't affect my definition of art at all. The art I mean can cost one hundred euros or one hundred thousand.

Ulrich Dietz I see. When art succeeds in calling into question or correcting my perception of something, it has managed to convey to me, or give me, something new. So in the best case does great art make the viewer more innovative and creative?

Tobias Rehberger Of course! It happens in increments, sometimes more subtly, sometimes more radically. A very important element is that you only become conscious of your own limitedness if you overcome it. Art is a wonderful vehicle for processes like these.

Ulrich Dietz Art extends consciousness?

Tobias Rehberger Yes, although consciousness sounds a little too psychological to me, and perception too scientific. When I had the first Sony Walkman in the 1980s, and was suddenly able to listen to music at the swimming pool and riding my bike, that also enriched my world. That too was a new moment you could physically experience.

Ulrich Dietz The new things an engineer is capable of creating in his defined environment—always one step after another, working empirically and in an evolutionary way—differ fundamentally from the new things artists or other creative professionals bring about. Such people are always jumping out of their formats. On the other hand I meet a lot of software engineers in the companies we work for, none of whom are capable of designing new products.

Tobias Rehberger Not a single one among a hundred engineers?

Ulrich Dietz Unfortunately not. But actually it would be easy. An example is Amazon's electronic reading device Kindle, on which you can digitally store books and read them. You could ask yourself, for example, what else can I do with it? Perhaps you'd come up with the idea that a doctor could store two thousand books on it and have his library permanently on hand in his surgery…Productive industry in particular finds it very difficult to get out of its straitjacket.

Tobias Rehberger The artist has the advantage of being his own client. You can think about everything, in contrast to the engineers at Daimler, who have their specifications.

Ulrich Dietz Companies usually only function with defined structures. These are necessary, but how do you implement new things despite them? You have to find points of intersection. This is why we have started an experiment in our subsidiary in Spain. We have seven hundred employees there who have all kinds of ideas that they'll unfortunately never be able to realize. These ideas are written up on our company Intranet—every which way. Later they become available to all employees in the entire company. But how do you direct creativity in order to keep it creative? Because in principle it's desirable to have the res publica—among it as many potential clients as possible—participate actively.

Tobias Rehberger I see the problem that in this way the final result is the common denominator, which is the

John&
Paul&
Ringo&
George.

exact opposite of innovation. Quite a few companies ask users if they can envisage this or that product. And then fifty or a hundred ideas come together; some want something more angular, others something more colorful—and in the end you have a mainstream product with nothing new about it.

Ulrich Dietz You doubt whether exciting new products can come about with the support of the general public?

Tobias Rehberger If you involve too many people, the result is usually a compromise in which the ideas are inevitably leveled out. And you're also taking the premise that everyone is full of ideas. I have my doubts there.

Ulrich Dietz I see it differently. I think human beings are per se rich in ideas. It's a problem of education, which channels ideas and unfortunately often kills them. But actually every child is a little inventor.

Tobias Rehberger Creative per se? Then everyone would be an artist, as Joseph Beuys proposed.

Ulrich Dietz Hm, there are millions of artists, but only a few win through. Why, actually?

Tobias Rehberger In my opinion this is dependent on the particular zeitgeist. One artist fits in better than another. But in the course of history it's only what lasts beyond the various expiry dates of the zeitgeist that counts in the end.

Ulrich Dietz You once said: contemporary art is closer to the confusion in which I find myself. Can you describe what you mean more exactly?

Tobias Rehberger By confusion I mean that I don't believe in set patterns. So initially everything is, well, confusing. Art is the discipline that can most profoundly deal with this confusion.

Ulrich Dietz That's your advantage. Another statement stayed with me: you said that today everything can be material for art.

Tobias Rehberger That was about the freedom I claim. I don't understand, for example, why a piece of fabric and some slushy paint should have more or less to do with art than a packet of Q-Tips and a bunch of grapes. The art isn't in the material, but in how you put it together and what kind of light this throws on what has been taken for art up to now. That's what art is about, but it actually applies to all creative processes. Because there's nothing there hasn't already been. In principle even the iPod was there at the beginning of creation. That's why everything is material, no matter whether it's a thought or a fab-

ric, it's just always combined differently. That's what constitutes the new.

Ulrich Dietz With artists it comes about single-handedly. In other areas through teamwork. Now you're running a kind of company with around a dozen employees. How does the idea input work in your studio?

Tobias Rehberger I'm the one who thinks up things and brings together particular ideas. My employees look over these conceptual sketches, research them and then realize them technically. Our collaboration is very close—not like in a company, where the head often doesn't know what the tail is doing anymore. But we too have loss of friction and turbulence. Which can have their good sides. I'm a big fan of productive misunderstandings, as I call them.

Ulrich Dietz They can sometimes give rise to the most wonderful things!

Tobias Rehberger Right. Sometimes someone does something wrong, but I think it fits the design better and I take it on. I often notice that in view of the countless mass-produced consumer items I crave a certain imperfection.

Ulrich Dietz Do you mean originality, craftsmanship?

Tobias Rehberger Yes. Manufacture, handiwork. Although my relationship to it is ambivalent. Take my old radio, for example. It constantly needs repairing, but it still has something I'm more fond of than with any high-tech gadget. Although of course I value and need those products. But for me they only function on my perceptive periphery. Things with small flaws and irregularities are at the centre of my gaze.

Ulrich Dietz Because they are more haptic and sensuous?

Tobias Rehberger And more complex.

Ulrich Dietz You're right. I experience this in our Stuttgart house, which was built in the 1950s. It's more…

Tobias Rehberger …it's easier to settle into.

Ulrich Dietz Exactly. In that context another sentence of yours occurs to me which needs a little more explanation: the new becomes a kind of guideline or navigation point for the old and forgotten.

Tobias Rehberger When did I say that? OK, the new puts the old in a new light. The car made the carriage into a different object from what it had used to be. Against the background of our computers a handwritten letter has a different significance today than previously.

Ulrich Dietz For sure, the new is defined through the old. As an artist, do you have ideas everywhere and all the time?

Tobias Rehberger I think so. But I don't realize them all, by any means. And I don't realize them in a linear fashion either. On the contrary, sometime I carry them around inside me for years until they're ripe.

Ulrich Dietz Your approach to a subject is obviously diametrically opposed to that of an entrepreneur. The entrepreneur wants to produce an ashtray, for example. His innovative input consists of deciding what material it should be made from, how many should be produced, and so on. You, on the other hand, begin with ideas that sometimes seem almost erroneous. As with the vase portraits you produced of your friends.

Tobias Rehberger The vase! For a while my thoughts revolved around this object and its universal laws, and why people put flowers in different kinds of vases. Most of us choose flowers for more or less unconscious reasons. At some point I was able to distill a particular typology of individuality from these observations. And because I've always been interested in the portrait as a genre, I came up with the idea of defining artist friends of mine as vases, and of asking them to define themselves as flowers. The work came from all this. It also—as always with me—includes the question of the definition of art in general. For the vase is only a Rehberger sculpture when it contains the right flowers. And if it doesn't, what is it then? Only semi-art? These indeterminacy principles are an essential part of the works.

Ulrich Dietz Entrepreneurs sometimes also start out with ideas that seem strange to other people. But in the end you need a product that can be bought by as many consumers as possible.

Tobias Rehberger You've achieved something if the work is interesting to even a single person. And also if it's only interesting to you yourself.

Ulrich Dietz Hence your unmistakable handwriting.

Tobias Rehberger That's the result of my way of perceiving people and things differently from others. Only gradually does this give rise to a particular aesthetic vocabulary. But I don't vary it according to a particular pattern; it's continually reforming itself. It's not about effect, but insight.

Ulrich Dietz As with Andy Warhol?

Tobias Rehberger Yes, or with Gerhard Richter. He started out with motifs he painted from newspapers, and then there were the blurred abstractions, the indistinct landscapes, portraits, the gray series. At a cursory glance these works don't seem to belong together, but if you look more closely you soon discover the core around which it all revolves, and you can see how Richter approaches this core in many different ways. With me it's the same, and it's always about shifting perspectives, breaking the mold.

Ulrich Dietz Perhaps new things need exactly this core, this obsession about something, this search.

Tobias Rehberger Although I don't believe in solutions, only in the approach to solutions. That's the difference from the entrepreneur, who has to generate solutions and added value.

Ulrich Dietz Perhaps we should differentiate between an entrepreneur and a manager. The entrepreneur enjoys inventing new things, playfully exploring new things. That's how the products come about that are useful to many people, who want them for this reason.

Tobias Rehberger Although some entrepreneurs produce articles they only sell to an exclusive clientele, and others concentrate on discount commerce. Why one person does one thing and another does something else usually has to do with aesthetic preferences.

Ulrich Dietz We do both. We produce products that bring in a safe income, and others that we decide to go ahead with although we don't earn any money with them at first.

Tobias Rehberger For example?

Ulrich Dietz There's a project with a trade-fair company. Increasingly fewer exhibitors and visitors go to exhibitions—for reasons of cost, among other things. How can you win them back? By holding out the prospect of an added value from their attendance. For example, if you're going to a particular fair, you can find out which of your acquaintances or potential clients are also attending. So apart from your other duties you can also use it to make contacts and appointments.

Tobias Rehberger A kind of Twitter or Facebook for trade-fairs?

Ulrich Dietz Right. One of our teams is currently working on a concept and extrapolating solutions from which a new technical product to bring about this intercommunication could perhaps emerge. The classical procedure would be to ask trade-fair companies what they need and to respond with the appropriate services. But you're only innovative if you develop a different approach. The essence of our conversation is that you utilize things differently by asking what you might otherwise do with them. As an entrepreneur I like to throw a pebble into the pond and see what waves it makes. And doesn't every artist aim to provoke? I'm thinking of your teacher Martin Kippenberger, for example. Or was that an expression of his way of living?

Tobias Rehberger I think more the latter. That's one of those big misunderstandings, the idea that artists want to provoke. I've never thought about how people might react—more about how I react. We artists also throw pebbles into the pond, but not to provoke scandals. We want to find out whether what then happens counts for us or not. Even Kippenberger never did anything for the sake of sensation, but always from the need to find out something for himself. And this was what he gave to his students—me, for example—as a creative legacy.

Ulrich Dietz I'm not very far away from that as an entrepreneur. I too am driven to do what I do by my own problems. Finally I would like to ask you the eternal question: What is good art for you?

Tobias Rehberger For me it's art that enables me, after I've seen and understood it, to think differently about art, and my previous perspectives on it. But also to think differently about life and the world as a whole. Great art changes my life.

Roberto Stern

"Never forget your roots, because they lead to the future."

Roberto Stern

Like all *Cariocas*, Roberto Stern loves his native city, Rio de Janeiro, for its incomparable sensory beauty. The eldest of four sons, he was born there in 1961 into the dynasty of one of the leading jewelry companies in the world. His German father, Hans, emigrated from Essen with his parents in 1939, fleeing the National Socialist regime of terror. After the Second World War, the company grew from nothing to one of the most successful in the industry. When Roberto took over the boss's job in 1995, he renovated the company from the ground up. Not only did he develop a chic, simple logo but he also hired famous designers for extravagant signature collections. The H. Stern team gets its inspiration from artists and choreographers, and recently the star architect Oscar Niemeyer designed a collection. It is a cult brand for Hollywood stars.

After weeks of spring rain, the sun is finally shining again in Munich, which is appropriate for our visit with the Brazilian Roberto Stern. On the roof terrace of the Blue Spa at the Bayerischer Hof, every seat is occupied—good thing we made a reservation. The jeweler is on a European tour, visiting his stores; the luxurious flagship store in Munich is right next door. Every sentence makes clear just how much he loves his profession. Not a second passes without him thinking about a new collection with his team, leafing through countless magazines for inspiration, or studying the sales numbers for his company—no getting around that. But the key to success, he reveals, is women. His biggest challenge is constantly reconsidering them and their psyches.

Ulrich Dietz While I was going over your biography I was reminded of my own family history. My grandfather was also in the jewelry business. He left Germany in the 1920s and went to Italy to set up a company there. My family still runs a jewelry company, but in Germany at the moment business in this field is generally modest. Most firms are small family concerns—often without enough equity and unfortunately not at all in touch with current trends. Your company H. Stern, however, is world famous, active in nineteen countries and economically successful. It's a global brand which is continuing to develop because it combines tradition with innovation. Is it this combination that is able to regenerate the luxury product?

Roberto Stern You're addressing an essential aspect there. In a field like ours you do in fact have to continue reinterpreting the past. Never forget your roots, because they lead to the future. That's our credo.

Ulrich Dietz Although your roots are relatively young.

Roberto Stern That's right, but our country is also relatively young. My father Hans, who was born in Essen in 1922, came to Rio de Janeiro in 1939 at the age of sixteen. He used to ride on horseback out to the garimpeiros, the prospectors for precious stones, because there were scarcely any paved roads in those days. He began trading in colored gemstones—aquamarines, tourmalines, amethysts and topaz—and he discovered a gap in the market. These stones had been badly neglected until then by a market that concentrated on diamonds and oriental stones like rubies, sapphires and emeralds. And because the business flourished, he founded an office for precious stones in 1945, and in 1949 the first shop in the port of Rio de Janeiro, where the American cruise ships docked. The tourists from the United States were such good customers that in 1960 he was able to open his first branch in New York.

Ulrich Dietz He expanded into new countries even then, as a relatively small company.

Roberto Stern Yes, my father wanted the visitors to be able to buy jewelry at home, not only in Brazil. He was also ahead of his time in that he focused as far as possible on a tailor-made service from the very beginning. As early as 1952 he began to offer tours of his workshops, which encouraged customer commitment. He was a pioneer, but he was always modest about it. He maintained a very discreet kind of luxury to the very end.

Ulrich Dietz I loved reading in an article that your father drove an old Volkswagen for years. One day I too sold all my prestige cars, and since then I've driven a VW Golf. It's perfectly all right for town, and on business I go by train or fly.

Roberto Stern My father had his own philosophy. He said you could certainly have a villa, a yacht, or an art collection, but not a big expensive car. Because this would give rise to too much social envy. He even forbade his managers to drive limousines. I too rely on the elegance of self-confident understatement.

Ulrich Dietz You've inherited the visionary spirit of your father. What did you learn from him?

Roberto Stern Very much. Above all the courage to go in new directions. My father undoubtedly developed a business model that set standards in the jewelry industry. This included an international certificate of guarantee for the jewels, and his own gemological laboratory, in which every precious stone and every metal was tested for purity and quality according to the standards of the GIA, the Gemological Institute of America. In 1964, *Time* magazine enthusiastically called him the "King of diamonds and gems." So it was difficult to grow into his shoes. In that year, by the way, he opened his first shop in Europe—in Frankfurt.

Ulrich Dietz How were you able to gain your own profile, as the son of such a dominant father figure?

Roberto Stern My father gave me the opportunity to develop my own ideas. That was his gift to me. And his strengths were also in other areas than mine, which was a great relief to me, so I was gradually able to emerge from his shadow. While he placed great value on the size, color and purity of the stones, I was more devoted to their unique beauty. For me the secret of perfect jewels lies in the naturalness and variety of their forms. My father was more interested in perfection. And while he didn't focus on design, for me it was at the centre of my work from the outset.

Ulrich Dietz But hadn't he also emphasized design?

Roberto Stern You're right. He took a step in that direction in 1959, when he organized Brazil's first fashion show of jewelry. Later he took part in international exhibitions, and in the 1980s he introduced a Catherine Deneuve collection, inscribed with the initials CD, inspired by Luis Buñuel's *Belle de Jour*. It was a runaway success! And I built on these ideas when I took over the directorship of the company in 1995.

Ulrich Dietz Did you want to do this as the eldest of four sons from the very beginning?

Roberto Stern No, on the contrary. When I was still a teenager I fought against it with every fiber of my being. We children hardly ever saw our father. He more or less lived in his office, and we experienced the company as competition. I did study business sciences, but I also read Karl Marx and when I was twenty I went to a kibbutz in Israel. So I rebelled against my father as he had rebelled against his. My grandfather was an engineer and raised my father very strictly. He had to learn to type at the age of twelve, and later to play the accordion. He hated playing folk music with family and friends. Ironically, though, the instrument later became part of his seed capital when he sold it for two hundred dollars in 1945.

Ulrich Dietz Did he encourage you in your ideas and aims?

Roberto Stern Well, he found it very difficult to pay compliments and admit feelings. In this way he was, if you'll excuse me, typically German. Luckily for me I'm more extrovert.

Ulrich Dietz I'm very familiar with that kind of behavior. We have a saying: "It's enough praise not to be scolded."

Roberto Stern That's exactly how he was! But on the other hand open to my experiments.

Ulrich Dietz What were some of your experiments?

Roberto Stern Taking over the directorship in 1995 was in many ways a decisive break, not only because it represented a change of generations. But don't think the door to the director's office stood open—I had to fight my way in! Since I'd been on the kibbutz, which had been very disillusioning, I no longer believed in a classless society. So I decided to enter the company.

Ulrich Dietz Was your apprenticeship difficult?

Roberto Stern It was austere. I began as a messenger, and then I was allowed to run a small branch. But at least I got to know our company from the bottom up. In 1991 I took over the Brazil operation and reorganized the stock, distribution and production. Today our goldsmiths and craftspeople all work in the same workshop, from the smelter to the jewel cutter and jewel setter to the polisher. Every step in the production process is transparent, which makes us much more effective. But in 1995 we were in crisis. The management had an average age of seventy, turnover was dropping, our market share was stagnant.

Ulrich Dietz Was it about saving H. Stern?

Roberto Stern It was about a complete renewal, at least. We had to rejuvenate at all levels—in the staff, but also in our collections. That was when we turned ourselves into a house that set trends in jewelry design.

Ulrich Dietz Do you design new collections yourself?

Roberto Stern I express my ideas through words or pictures to the in-house design team. They implement my ideas for our signature collections—collections with thematic accents, like in the fashion world. A particular design appears in very different pieces, like a leitmotif. Customers can choose from various series and don't have to buy sets like in the old days—ensembles of a ring, earrings or necklace in the same style.

Ulrich Dietz What's the innovative thing about that?

Roberto Stern We enable our customers, above all our female customers—for it's women who wear jewelry—to emphasize their own individual style. This is done best through pieces with a delicate and subtle luxury. Actually I spend my whole time trying to find out how women think, and I often browse for days through countless international magazines. Because I'm convinced that the success of our company is largely dependent on women.

Ulrich Dietz And how do women think?

Roberto Stern They observe details and workmanship very exactly and love the not-so-conspicuous extras, like a concealed gem splinter, or the tiny stars engraved into the inside. Men, on the other hand, are more impressed by the amount of carats and the production techniques. They're more outwardly fixated.

Ulrich Dietz But isn't it above all men who buy jewelry for their wives and girlfriends?

Roberto Stern They do, but women increasingly choose their jewelry for themselves. And in doing so they enhance their self-esteem, especially through rings with large stones. One of our most successful collections ever was inspired by the Belgian-American fashion designer Diane von Furstenberg in 2004. This is jewelry for contemporary, liberated women. Earrings, massive bracelets and above all rings, set with colorful stones as big as chicken's eggs! Jewelry that gives you strength, magic and charisma. For von Furstenberg, jewelry is decoration, investment and weapon—a very modern definition, I think. Our collection sparked off a trend. It was widely imitated. We're now working with Diane on a new series, because the first one was so successful.

Ulrich Dietz So you're involved in a creative interchange with other disciplines. Does this lead to innovation?

Roberto Stern It certainly does. The cross-over of different artistic disciplines is essential for us to be able to continually reinvent ourselves as jewelry designers and to remain interesting to our clients. That's why I regularly commission artists from other fields to design jewelry for us—musicians, directors, dancers, choreographers. One of our most recent lines, for example, converts the archaic, erotic movements of the Brazilian dance company Grupo Corpo into very sensual, baroque jewelry. Our goldsmiths needed three years to hone their technique, but the result was worth the effort.

Ulrich Dietz What does innovation mean to you?

Roberto Stern Innovation gives us more freedom. But you don't have to reinvent your profession in order to be innovative. It's enough, for example, to take up a great historical style, such as art déco, and give it a contemporary touch. At H. Stern we don't only reflect our own roots, but also those of other cultures. We borrow from their creativity, adopt certain forms and merge them with our own aesthetic ideas.

Ulrich Dietz So for you the principle is constant change. Do your customers follow you wherever you go?

Roberto Stern They have up to now. Our regular customers still identify with our products. They expect us to bring fresh designs on to the market twice a year. We're also being noticed by new people, who become fans. People are looking for a change, entertainment, animation, stimulus. The search for the new is fundamental… The greatest resistance to the new is not among our customers, but within our company!

Ulrich Dietz That's a well-known fact to me. Resistance arises as soon as you leave the familiar paths. It continually astonishes me how unresponsively staff and management react to changes, even in dynamic modern companies. Always with the same arguments: we haven't got a budget for it, or the teams to implement it; there isn't a market. Working against this inertia is very tiring and time-consuming. At the moment I'm supporting a twenty-two-year-old who has founded a fashion label on the Internet which he also wants to build up into a social platform—Youdress.com. The idea is simple: people open their wardrobes, and sell and swap items of clothing with other users. This kind of involvement is way outside our main business, so it was even more tricky to enthuse my colleagues for the investment.

Taking risks and developing new things is increasingly difficult for people in companies. I see this as an alarming development.

Roberto Stern It certainly is. Everyone complained when I slimmed down and modernized our antiquated elaborate logo; now everyone's got used to it, and there'd be an outcry if I changed it again.

Ulrich Dietz Group lethargy is widespread in all industries. Do all H. Stern's lines sell equally well? Don't you have the occasional flop?

Roberto Stern Unfortunately. The frustrating thing is that we can never really explain why our customers didn't go for a particular collection. Every single one of our pieces is excellently made and convincingly designed. A good example is our collaboration with the Brazilian star designers Fernando and Humberto Campana. I liked their slogan "Do lixo ao luxo," from garbage to luxury. We did everything right. It was an expensive production—but it didn't sell well. In the end we had to melt the collection down. My only explanation in retrospect is that the Campanas' designs perhaps seemed too masculine.

Ulrich Dietz There are no recipes for innovative design. A lot of managers need to grasp this at last. Mainstream and large profits are possible, but they destroy a company from within. This emphasis destroys innovation—and the company, in the long term. Instead we need to mix the established with the avant-garde, as you do. In the long run every company will grow in this way, in public perception and in the end in turnover and revenue.

Roberto Stern Exactly. It's about getting the right balance. Sometimes you have to be commercial and sell things that you yourself don't like. In the end the figures decide, which is why 80 percent of my time is unfortunately taken up with reading balance sheets and only 20 percent with creative adventures.

Ulrich Dietz Have you also had an economical campaign with an unexpectedly large success?

Roberto Stern That too. In 2001 I had a bad accident, when I fell six meters off a cliff while on holiday in Turkey. I spent eight months in hospital and had to have a great many operations, including a lot of dental treatments. This gave rise to the idea of setting up a dentist's chair in two shops in Rio. Customers could have a star, a flower or a lizard set into a front tooth. And people came in droves!

Ulrich Dietz A nice side effect. It must cut into your marketing budget a lot more to have Hollywood stars promoting your products at the Oscars ceremony. But it focuses considerable attention on your brand.

Roberto Stern It certainly helps us a great deal if Uma Thurman, Catherine Zeta-Jones or Scarlett Johansson wear our jewelry. We were the first ones in the industry to develop a celebrity concept, but now a lot of people are imitating us. I'm not sure how long this kind of advertising will still function.

Ulrich Dietz I'm sure you'll come up with something new. How many shops does H. Stern have around the world at the moment?

Roberto Stern There are 186. We have over three thousand people working for us. But at the moment we're tending to downsize. We're closing less profitable shops and reopening in other locations where we hope for more success. This is a continual process in retail, because the shops are very expensive and need to achieve a corresponding turnover.

Ulrich Dietz Where are your largest markets?

Roberto Stern In Latin America we're the number one, by a long way, and this market is growing. But we're also growing in the United States; we're about to open a shop in Las Vegas. Israel is also a big market for us, Europe less so. The brand only does really well in Portugal.

Ulrich Dietz Do you think this is because of the European competition from Cartier, Bulgari and co.?

Roberto Stern That might have something to do with it. Europe is still a challenge for us.

Ulrich Dietz Perhaps you could get a foothold in the continent via the watch market. This brings in a lot of money here.

Roberto Stern Perhaps, but the watch market is in fact very expensive. In Brazil only 5 percent of our turnover is in wristwatches. Who knows, perhaps our most recent collection with Oscar Niemeyer, the famous Brazilian architect, who is also much admired in Europe, will be successful. At the biblical age of 102 he has designed some wonderfully filigree, weightless jewelry for us, true to his motto "life is just a breath of air." The Brazilians can't get enough of these pieces, which they see as his legacy.

Peter Weibel

"Without the new, we would have no chance for survival."

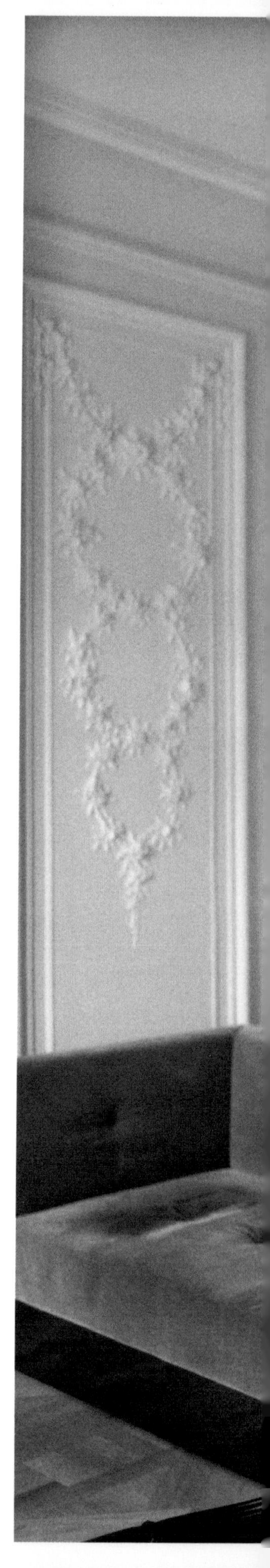

Peter Weibel

A former action artist who, at the height
of the student unrest of 1968, gave a diatribe
against the Austrian government while wearing a burning glove. Today Peter Weibel,
born in 1944 in Odessa, Ukraine, is one
of the most respected media theorists in
the world and an extremely wide-ranging
exhibition organizer. He studied French,
film, and comparative literature in Paris
and then literature, philosophy, medicine,
and mathematical logic in Vienna. After
his years in the circle of the Viennese
Actionists, in the 1970s Weibel became
more active teaching on the university level
and increasingly concentrated on media art.
He has curated numerous exhibitions and
since 1999 has been director of the Zentrum
für Kunst und Medientechnologie (ZKM)
in Karlsruhe.

An incomparable restaurant. The rococo spaces of Schloss Hohenheim, near Stuttgart, with its chased crystal chandeliers and gold-framed mirrors, which was once the love nest of Duke Carl Eugen von Württemberg and his mistresses, have housed Speisemeisterei since 2008, where chef Frank Oehler cooks in a Eurasian style. In the room with the fireplace Peter Weibel is leaning back into blue-gray velvet cushions. The interior is commandingly audacious, with its seating cubes of coral red velvet sofas, black lacquered coffee tables, and dark leather chairs. A sumptuous sense of aristocratic splendor meets the bourgeois fusion aesthetic of the twenty-first century; eighteenth-century Enlightenment encounters the enlightened third millennium. And we discover how beneficial the new can be to pleasure.

 How do you define the new?

 I think it's essential to use a new definition of new. On the one hand, the new signifies a danger, an upending of values, a break with tradition, for the new is measurable only in relation to tradition. On the other hand, the new is an imperative. It is a rule of both our economy and our culture that academics, artists, and entrepreneurs must invent new products, create new markets, and thereby inevitably break with traditions.

 What is your theory of the new?

 It is based on the future not being a disease to live in fear of. The new is not based on tradition, but on the future, and to that extent possesses a sort of function of messianic salvation. The new is awaited like a messiah who will free us from the misery of the present and of the past. Thus one cannot invent the light bulb (standing for the future) if one only aspires to improve the candle (as a symbol for the past). But what is fundamental: The new is always on its way.

 How is the new recognized?

 The question is not how, but when. What matters is recognizing it promptly. Yet most people are not prepared to recognize the new in its current form—namely, as the light bulb. They see only the past form, the candle. The new comes in a form that one does not recognize. This is the reason why it is rejected, even though people actually long for its arrival. This is the tragic dialectic of the new.

 Obviously you recognize the new promptly. How do you achieve that?

 I can grasp a situation on the basis of very few data points. With those data points, I can create a valid model of the facts, as with a puzzle. I need only to turn a map around to recognize the rest of the puzzle image. That is why I see the new earlier than others do. When I discover themes and needs more quickly than my fellow humans, I gain time. Someone who has a feel for the fine nuances can filter the data and trends quicker than others can. Yet of course it can happen that one will recognize a trend too early. Gorbachev was wrong: Life does not punish those who come too late. It punishes those who come too early.

 But what is the new new?

 At this point I should point out that the new is not always so new as it seems at first. In many cases, what goes into creating something new is distilling what is already known and joining it together with other things that are already known. The ability to rewrite the existing information is enough. Rewriting is the key word. Being creative means being able to rewrite.

 The new, in other words, must not push out the old. No one can invent a motor without knowing how to build it.

 That's how it is. It's also exciting to consider the relationship of the new to evolution. Evolution allows new things to arise through adaptation and selection. Not through upheaval or destruction, but through slow rewriting. The factor of time, out to eternity, plays a decisive role in amphibians turning into fish, then land animals, birds, mammals, primates. We can learn from evolution: Without the new, we would have no chance for survival and no future. Translated onto culture, this means: The people who make new things despite all obstacles are precious. They guarantee the survival of society. Each society lives only by the next society that is always creating the new. In this regard, the new is a priority of evolution.

 Otherwise we would be on the level of the dinosaurs. Humans apparently have a limitless drive to do new things.

 Exactly. But the new is often so radical that it triggers massive resistance. Every partisan of the new encounters the experience of having ideas while others have objections.

 You said it. Unfortunately, the majority of people want to keep to the status quo, even when it leads to their own ruin. Everything should stay the way it always was. A good example is the auto industry. It wants nothing so much as to live another century off internal combustion engines run on gas, and refuses to recognize the advantages of, or to see that the future lies in, electric motors.

 What stands behind this is the fear of losing familiar coordinates. I can understand this to an extent. People are afraid of the foreignness of the new.

 We have to alleviate their fear. Make clear to them that they will not lose anything by being curious and open, but indeed will make important gains, and that things will ultimately be better for everyone.

 Unfortunately, the dominant power structures are almost always hostile to innovation.

The resistance to the new is systemic. It is well known that every system seeks equilibrium, stability, the maintenance of the status quo. Therefore every change is regarded as destabilization, as a threat to the system, and the renewers are considered to be system destroyers. A dominant system only comes apart or implodes once a very large majority no longer profits from it. You may not believe it, but that even happens in art. Art in general is no more open to innovation than politics or business. I know what I'm talking about, having been an artist myself. In the 1960s, I was part of the circle of Vienna Actionists around Günther Brus, Hermann Nitsch, Rudolf Schwarzkogler, and Otto Muehl.

Ulrich Dietz In other words, you were one of those radicals who destroyed their icons, the heroes of art history. Is destruction a kind of creativity? An energy from which new things come about? Put another way, must one destroy the old on behalf of the new? Are revolutions innovative or destructive?

Peter Weibel Joseph Schumpeter, the Austrian economist, coined the term for the phenomenon you mention of "creative destruction." He believed that every innovation in the capitalist system is destructive. This is what gives the economy its dynamic in which new branches of economic activity drive out old ones. The old must vanish for the new to arise, a concept derived from the theory of evolution. What really matters, though, is to keep sounding out the relationship between the old and the new. It is helpful to hold onto the curiosity of a child. "Never lose a childlike wonder." Children are not yet conformist. Many inventors—has this struck you too?—retain childlike traits at an advanced age. This childlike openness to the new must be practiced throughout one's lifetime. For me, the greatest of the infantile revolutionaries was Jesus Christ.

Ulrich Dietz Excuse me?

Peter Weibel Wasn't it extremely childish to say, "Love thy neighbor as thyself?" Thus he broke through the principle of cause and effect! Instead of continuing the cycle of revenge, the "eye for an eye," he said: "If you strike me, I will not strike back, but instead turn the other cheek." His revolution was and is the most innovative that there has ever been. That is because he abolished the principle of sin. A new beginning is only possible if we do not count up, and demand a reckoning for, each other's mistakes.

Ulrich Dietz Why do many brilliant inventors fail?

Here I am not thinking of Jesus, in whom countless people have believed over the past two thousand years and because of whose message hundreds of thousands have massacred each other. But someone like Nikola Tesla, say, the Croatian who was the greatest competitor of Thomas Edison, the American who invented the light bulb. Tesla made alternating current feasible, but died in dire poverty in spite of all of his patents.

Peter Weibel An unappreciated genius, alas!

Ulrich Dietz As a media theorist, you know about the countless ways of manipulating both old and new media. The Internet strikes me as the one best situated to regulate itself.

Peter Weibel Absolutely: Messages distributed via Twitter and YouTube can be immediately corrected by users when they contain incorrect information. Nowhere are media manipulations more quickly corrected.

Ulrich Dietz That isn't quite right. Nowhere are manipulations so unimpeded as on the net. Fakings of every kind are possible and widespread. What is particularly popular is adopting an opponent's arguments into one's own position, thereby canceling them out.

Peter Weibel The net is ambiguous, like all phenomena of this earth. An example: In the democracies of global society, an increasing number of people no longer feel themselves adequately represented. The net is increasingly becoming their platform. Magazines and newspapers once espoused the interests of the people who were not represented by the parties. That is why those publications were called critical. Today magazines and newspapers stand for dominant power relationships. Thus people now represent themselves on the Internet. That is to say, they make their own opinions. Their opinions are not shaped by a tabloid newspaper. New technologies, from the mobile telephone to the PC—not for nothing is it called the personal computer—allow for an inconceivable individualization and personalization. No one has yet mastered this, to be sure. This is why phenomena as extreme as 9/11 and the bloodbath of the Winnenden school shooting are possible. Individuals can terrorize the whole world. Again, what matters here is to learn how to handle the new. The childlike openness to the new requires lifelong practice.

Ulrich Dietz Will the virtualization of society through the Web's unlimited possibilities gradually displace esteem for the real?

Peter Weibel This is an extremely important achievement of our culture. Nature knows no museum. For us, the museum is the physically palpable, corporeally walkable, sensual treasure chamber of our cultural memory. Without museums, archives, and libraries, our Gothic altars and the knowledge of them would long since have perished.

Ulrich Dietz Another reason for the existence of museums is that human desire to learn. Man wishes to improve himself and his surroundings, and for this he needs connections to prior achievements.

Peter Weibel Right. Nature has no need for Noah's ark. We need it, though, not only to save ourselves and our culture, but nature as well, because without nature we could not survive. Unfortunately, most of those who are responsible for culture incline to only wanting to preserve the old.

Ulrich Dietz An eternal dilemma. There is a lack of balance, of mixing. But why? Because the people who are responsible for making investments in the field of new media do not yet understand them. Thus they cling solely to tradition.

Peter Weibel Sad but true. This is the source of vicious circles of self-fulfilling prophecies. People confirm their own prejudices and their own ignorance. The absence of education is usually complemented by the presence of self-delusion.

Ulrich Dietz Here again, what matters is to intelligently connect the two poles—the virtual and the real—and to use the one for the other. Thanks to digitalization, we can still do everything at the same time across the globe.

Peter Weibel Anything, anytime, anybody. That is the core of the digital revolution.

Ulrich Dietz Before we get too euphoric: What the present really lacks are new contents, and with them a new ethics.

Peter Weibel Exactly. But where will these new contents come about? Above all in niches, I think.

Ulrich Dietz How can we successfully meld these niches and the mainstream, new and old energies? A key question.

Peter Weibel In just this lies the achievement of our culture. It will leave behind as many plural worlds as possible. Therefore we must defend the capacity of these parallel worlds to be joined together. And new technologies and media that are transgender, transethnic, and transreligious help us to do this. When I board a plane, it doesn't matter whether the pilot is a Muslim, a Jew, or a Christian, a man or a woman, a Brazilian or a Swede. They all have to follow the same instructions to land safely. Technology is a universal language.

Ulrich Dietz Things only get complicated outside of technologies, in real life. When, for example, imagined enemies clash. We know that fundamentalism is anti-Enlightenment, and that fanatical ideologies only allow for one-sided, censored channels of information.

Peter Weibel For that reason, we must devote ourselves first and foremost to the ability of the many parallel worlds to be joined together, through communication, through dialogue, and through the transmission of knowledge.

Ulrich Dietz Looking at the world of Twitter and Facebook, one wonders sometimes why humanity has this ceaseless need to send messages.

Peter Weibel It is our deepest anthropological constant. Even animals have to communicate constantly to survive. It is the conditio sine qua non. The more opportunities and means a human has to communicate, the more frequently he will do so. We are now living in a paradise of multiple communication. Everyone, and children in particular, can say on a great diversity of channels: "I am."

Ulrich Dietz Doesn't it depend on which level one secures one's own self on? And that would bring us back to the question of new contents. To always be buffeted about by the same confessional trailer trash on every channel and in every kind of show—that can't be it. But who decides what "trash" really is?

Peter Weibel An important comment. The exact sciences contain clear criteria for what is quality and what isn't. But the criteria for humanities and the arts aren't clear.

Ulrich Dietz But when someone puts music, movies, literature, or art on the Internet, the res publica, the people, vote on their acceptance and attractiveness.

Peter Weibel What does that have to do with quality?

Ulrich Dietz When economic success is what matters, quality isn't the question any more.

Peter Weibel On the contrary! Because a canon of values stands behind everything—regardless of whether popular or elite contents are transported. Even hit songs and kitsch novels are constructed according to rules that arose outside the medium.

Ulrich Dietz I am convinced that, in the future as well as the present, people will long for a substance and quality that can only fully develop outside of the instant medium of the Internet—namely, in real spaces. What I find fascinating all the same is how today, on the web, new markets can arise and became sales successes without advertising of any kind. The time needed for such markets to collapse, to be sure, can be extremely brief.

Peter Weibel And why? What is missing is expertise! We need experts who will pay attention, including on the Internet, to maintaining the standards of the various disciplines. Otherwise, the risk looms of a total collapse of culture and spirit.

Ulrich Dietz How innovative are experts?

Peter Weibel Neither more nor less than everyone else. The ability to be creative, and thereby the ability to think of and implement new things, relates to a specific psychological makeup. Say, for example, that someone is influenced by the absence of a father, as I have been. It is highly likely that, later in life, he or she will choose a constellation that repeats the pattern of the absence of close attachment figures. This elementary disposition also appears in a sublimated form, of which I myself am an example. When reading Sigmund Freud's treatise *Civilization and Its Discontents,* I chanced upon the sentence, "Writing is the medium of absence." I was electrified at once, assuredly in stark contrast to the thousands who had read the essay before me. I read on: "Technology continues writing," and concluded at once, "A-ha, technology is the medium of absence. It brings us near to what is absent, and that is the reason for the terms tele-vision, tele-phonics." I had already found an important building block for my media theory.

Ulrich Dietz That is a magnificent description of how a new idea arises that can change consciousness! But to return one more time to art and artists. Aren't they the best sensors for, and thus the mirror of, society?

Peter Weibel Yes. Art is society's alarm system. In art, even psychoses and neurotic structures are considered valid up to a point. The artist can say that he is working from an inner compulsion and drive. Indeed, it is expected of him. Here I am thinking of Joseph Beuys and his credo: "Show your wound!"

Ulrich Dietz Are artists the shamans of society, society's alternate world?

Peter Weibel Precisely. Society needs them, and therefore they are accorded a broad scope in which to realize their creativity on behalf of the rest of the community.

Ulrich Dietz That's called the division of labor. But I am convinced that those on the workers' side, the artisans, employees, bankers, managers and entrepreneurs, long to abandon their own uniformity. They want to understand what the impalpable things are that artists make.

Peter Weibel It is unfortunate that the sides continue to be too divided. They must be mixed together a great deal more, since that is how new things will come about. To do this, to be sure, people have to be taught to break free from the conformity dictated to them by their education. Relatively few people dare to defend themselves. It is the development of a higher level of narcissistic self-love that makes it possible for people to defend themselves. Those people then assert their creativity and, in the best-case scenario, assert themselves even within conformity.

Ulrich Dietz Innovation is the real motor of our society, and thus also of our economy. The drive to create new things. To make products and services better!

Peter Weibel Innovation makes us ready for the future. We must fight for it with pleasure.

Alasdhair Willis

"It's about character today."

Alasdhair Willis

His life is a success story. Born in North Yorkshire in 1970, the youngest of four children of an entrepreneur and a physiotherapist, Alasdhair Willis studied painting and art theory at the Slade School of Fine Art in London. With the journalist Tyler Brulé, he cofounded the lifestyle magazine *Wallpaper** in 1996, which quickly became the style bible for the creative elite. Two years later, they sold the magazine for around two million dollars and founded the design agency Wink Media, which Brulé now runs alone. Willis went independent with the creative agency Announcement. Married to the fashion designer Stella McCartney, Willis founded Established & Sons in 2005. The company, which works with star designers such as Zaha Hadid and up-and-coming talent such as Maarten Baas, produces, distributes, and presents design.

How else could the design expert of the scene look than very British
in the best sense? His suit reflects casual understatement; the spaces of
his showroom-gallery for Established & Sons possess the subversively
chic that suggests cult appeal. Every piece of furniture is presented
as if it were an art object, but without actually claiming to be one.
Alasdhair Willis has that certain something that cannot be learned.
His style is not stylish; rather, it results from a precise knowledge of the
material with which he is working. He did not simply study the codes
of beauty and aesthetics as a theorist but also tried them out as an artist.
He knows that class comes from classic and that the new is founded
in tradition. He formulates his sentences eloquently, with a flawless
Oxford accent.

Ulrich Dietz Almost everyone likes the new. However, it also means change, and most people are afraid of that. That paradox is the point of departure for our book. You, by contrast, state totally fearlessly that you are starting something new because it makes you happy. Was it always that way?

Alasdhair Willis Yes. Originally, I wanted to be an artist. At the Slade School of Fine Art in London from 1989 to 1994, I studied painting and the critical theory of the French post-structuralists, above all the writings of Jean Baudrillard, Jacques Derrida, Michel Foucault, and Roland Barthes. It was a time when artists were beginning to engage intensely with the commercial side of their work. In parallel with their works, they developed marketing strategies; famously, the most brilliant example was Damien Hirst, one of the Young British Artists. At the time I left art school, I was convinced that whatever I did, it would be marketable. I wanted to do something that would immediately be visible, something that would be influential and communicative. I happened to meet the journalist Tyler Brûlé, and because I love magazines, we started *Wallpaper** in 1996.

Ulrich Dietz The style bible that revolutionized the lifestyle of the creative elite in the 1990s. How did you finance the magazine?

Alasdhair Willis The first four issues we produced largely with our own funds; a year later, we sold it to Time Warner for a little less than two million dollars, and in 1998 we invested the money in the design agency Wink Media, which Tyler now runs on his own as Winkreative. I then set up Announcement, an exclusive brand and creative consultancy, working with clients such as Adidas and Estée Lauder.

Ulrich Dietz You founded Established & Sons in 2005. Was this switch from a magazine to a company that produces, distributes, and exhibits furniture design by avant-garde designers a difficult one?

Alasdhair Willis On the contrary, it was a very natural one, because I never saw any difference between publishing a magazine, consulting, or running a design company. The creative aspect is always the same: I sit in the studio and write the first letter on a piece of paper, or draw the first line. There is an idea but no concept. Gradually, something takes shape, becomes more visible, and at some point, weeks or months later, it suddenly has the precisely outlined form of a new project, of a new company.

This process of transformation is the most exciting part. Going through it gives me energy, motivates me again and again.

Ulrich Dietz It is true, the first creative phase is the most emotional one, the happiest one, and I felt the same thing when I founded my companies.

Alasdhair Willis I try to communicate this pioneering spirit to my teams as well. To make clear to them that their ability to innovate is the foundation of the company's success.

Ulrich Dietz Do you profit from your experience in the media industry?

Alasdhair Willis Very much so! At first we published an online magazine, and recently we began printing it as well. I definitely would like to continue being involved in publishing, as someone who thinks about his business, not just as a furniture manufacturer, but as a design company. For that, you need a voice that is heard in various media and across a wide variety of platforms—and right now we are building a new one. We invite influential people from various industries and creative scenes to dinners, each of which focuses on a theme. We broadcast the events live on the Web and on television. Because we are not solely a furniture manufacturer, but rather a design brand.

Ulrich Dietz You are transferring media communication to a brand. That is indeed an interesting approach!

Alasdhair Willis Thanks. Whenever you start a company, you send out a message. You want to reach listeners who, you hope, will someday become consumers. The crucial thing is that the message is formulated and illustrated as clearly as possible. If it succeeds at that, there is a high probability a company will be successful.

Ulrich Dietz So at first it is about building a brand, since lots of people offer beautiful design objects. Because you initially focus on having a strong brand strategy, you get people to identify with your label and that is why they buy your products.

Alasdhair Willis Exactly. Although the one will not work without the other. Our brand is special. So we are building it around the success and quality of designers' personalities. It is, if you will, a collection of individuals, not of objects. All the designers with whom I work contribute their own unique style.

Ulrich Dietz A creativity network?

Alasdhair Willis More like a laboratory to foster individual creativity. I give designers an opportunity to pursue what interests them. Established & Sons is a model that never existed before us. Until now, things have been produced according to rational criteria such as whether it fits into a certain genre, a certain aesthetic, a certain kind of marketing. By contrast, I am developing our brand around individuals. The industry hardly understood our approach, but our customers did. Because that is how we all live, after all; as individuals we all have a point of view but might not know it. As such, we encourage our clients to create their own lives.

Ulrich Dietz I see it that way too. Every consumer designs his or her own existence, seeking change, a mix of stimuli. It seems to me that is the only perspective from which you can develop new things today, in all fields.

Alasdhair Willis Exactly. Today's aesthetic innovations also come from artists who work across boundaries. For example, Zaha Hadid, who comes out of architecture but also designs great furniture, and now fashions as well. We work closely together with her but also with designers from the other end of the spectrum, such as Jasper Morrison, whose uncompromising modern aesthetic we admire.

Ulrich Dietz I am thinking of Tom Ford and his model of an integrated luxury brand. At Gucci and now with his own label as well, Tom Ford adds one product after the other, from bags to glasses and perfume, all under the same label. Would that be a strategy for you?

Alasdhair Willis No. That was a tactic that worked great in the 1990s. Everything was concentrated on the personality of the designer, as was already the case with Gianni Versace and Giorgio Armani. I have my doubts that this concept, as successful as it once was, can still be successful today. How can one individual do justice to all my demands? The star as a figure of integration has lost a lot of authority.

Ulrich Dietz Why?

Alasdhair Willis Because people are looking for a variety of aesthetic styles today, not always brand loyalty in the form of identifying with a dominant figure. Individuals seek the authenticity of objects and experience, not the image of the label. At Established & Sons, we now work with twenty-eight designers. There are exceptions, of course, and brand worship does exist for the likes of Apple.

Ulrich Dietz Are you more a businessman or a curator?

Alasdhair Willis It is difficult for me to draw a line. My business is my creativity. Creativity has to be for a market, otherwise it is lost. For us, things just work out.

Ulrich Dietz Perhaps also because your customers have a certain aesthetic background. Aren't they often people from the art scene, such as collectors?

Alasdhair Willis Yes, absolutely. To understand our brand, you have to have a certain sensibility. You have to understand that design is more than applied art. It is an element of a certain lifestyle, an attitude that is communicated through aesthetics. We want to make a relevant contribution to the culture of our time.

Ulrich Dietz The current cross-over in aesthetic disciplines fascinates me. For example, I think of the German artist Tobias Rehberger, who sees himself as a sculptor but creates sculptures that look like design objects, and also function in a way that they are meant to be used.

Alasdhair Willis All artists want to cross boundaries and not be categorized. They want to explore and see how far they can go. It is a godsend to be able to work in their experimental whirlpool.

Ulrich Dietz In fact, the creativity of our century thus far seems to consist of a constant remix and sampling of ideas. Who is actually the star of Established & Sons, the designer or the brand?

Alasdhair Willis Good question. The focus is on the designer. But the platform, the brand, has to deliver perceived value as well. It is a balancing act, especially with respect to the next generation of designers we work with. For them especially, the brand has to be strong in order to offer a forum to promote young talent.

Ulrich Dietz How do you choose the next generation?

Alasdhair Willis I feel it in my gut. Whether established or at the start of a career, Established & Sons is a guarantee of innovative, high-quality design.

Ulrich Dietz Do you often produce prototypes and objects in small runs then?

Alasdhair Willis With unique objects and limited editions, we can turn a profit more quickly, which we then invest in making mass-produced objects. As a rule, you need three or more like four years before a piece can penetrate the mass market. We have shortened that time, following the example of the fashion industry. We introduce a product, then aim to quickly distribute and get into the market place.

 How quickly?

 Within about two or three months, is always our goal.

 It is a question of financing. To achieve that tempo, you have to manufacture in advance, not after an order has come in, as is usually done.

 Yes. That's also why we do small editions that bring liquidity faster. But there is a more fundamental reason: editions enable our designers to fail sometimes. The industry can not tolerate that, but it is crucial. Anyone who cannot fail cannot succeed either.

 And cannot be innovative. Do you consider design an art, as many people do?

 No, on the contrary. I draw a clear line. I would never show sculpture or painting. We represent designers, not artists, although we have and are working with some big artists. But even with them, we are producing design, not sculpture. That is the only way we can retain control. For example, we watch carefully where the pieces go and how we place them. That is particularly important for our young designers and their careers. We make sure they don't do too much—a mistake they are often inclined to make, but which can cause them to burn out quickly.

 Where do you see the next trends in design?

 The megatrend in all fields is sustainability. It is about credibility, about being true to yourself, about authenticity. Marketing it via stars and celebrities, as fashion houses still do—unfortunately the ones here are still hopelessly out of date—is no longer effective, as I said. Or not effective enough. Customers are looking for content, not surface. They are looking for brands they can believe in; they want truth, not illusion. That is our message as well.

 A fundamental change in consciousness is underway.

 Exactly. It is about character today. Products have to have a long life again. The age of the disposable society is in question; people want things to last. They prefer to buy a jacket for a thousand euros that they can keep for thirty years rather than ten for a hundred euros that fall apart after a year. Which is, by the way, also the better environmental investment.

 I agree with you. We see that in a lot of sectors: consumers are clearly thinking more about quality again.

 Quality of craftsmanship, and hence much more durable but also a more sustainable aesthetic. Objects that have that kind of value tell a story. People appreciate that, objects with a history, with substance. Like our products have, for example.

 Which design markets are strongest now?

 Europe is still a little weak, after the economic meltdown of 2008. On the other hand, the Brazilian market seems to be exploding, and the Middle East is also developing rapidly. China is very dynamic too. Although the Chinese continue to copy. But even in China, gradually there are more people searching for originals, who are also prepared to pay for it. India is not yet that far along, and Japan is a disaster at the moment.

 How did you come up with the name Established & Sons?

 On the one hand, it was supposed to signal an awareness of tradition and to recall a fruitful period in British manufacturing; on the other hand, it was also supposed to point to the future of the next generation, i. e. Sons. It was one of the rare last-minute inspirations. The typography plays with opposites. For Established, I used Helvetica, a typeface associated with a modern aesthetic, and for Sons, a neo-classical Antiqua, which radiates retro flair. But it is precisely this contradictory dovetailing that makes it attractive.

 Not for the first time in our conversation, I see that the secret of what you do seems to be that you think like an artist.

 It is true. And yours?

 Perhaps that I am curious about the new.

Ken Yeang

"Nature is the greatest inventor of all time."

Ken Yeang

He became famous as a pioneer of the bioclimatic skyscraper, but the Malaysian architect Ken Yeang is much more than that: he is the radical intellectual force and master planner of a green future. Born in Penang in 1948, he studied architecture in London from 1966 to 1971 and from 1971 to 1975 at Wolfson College of Cambridge University. Together with Tengku Robert Hamzah, a prince of the Malaysian royal family, immediately on completing his studies he cofounded the firm T. R. Hamzah & Yeang in Kuala Lumpur. From there and from London, where he runs a sister company, Yeang plans and realizes model ecological buildings worldwide and is also much in demand as a master planner for urban development.

At first he is restrained, almost a little shy. The café in London's West End where we are scheduled for breakfast is closed this Saturday morning, so we go to the self-service snack bar next door. Over tea, coffee, and a couple of sandwiches, the architect with a timelessly young face becomes increasing lively; by the end, he is even amusing us with cheery jokes about talking dogs and singing plants and inviting us to join him for lunch at his favorite Chinese place. But first we travel to London's Hyde Park, not far from the Serpentine Gallery, where his portrait photograph is to be shot. Yeang is in a talkative mood, telling us about his wife and children and his friend Jimmy Choo, the famous shoe designer. For the portrait he choses the largest tree he can find, closes his eyes, and spreads out his arms: an eco pioneer in his element, in nature.

Ulrich Dietz Mr. Yeang, you are considered a pioneer of ecological design and master planning, and, together with your business partner, Tengku Robert Hamzah, you have realized many high-rises, commercial complexes, residential buildings, and entire master plans throughout the world. You design architecture that combines urbanism with bioclimatic, energy-saving, and ecological principles. Where are you building right now?

Ken Yeang I have projects in UK, China, Hong Kong, Korea, Singapore, Malaysia, India, Kazakhstan, Uzbekistan, Turkey, and Canada. In London, we are building the extension of the Great Ormond Street Children's Hospital which will include two new buildings. These are over eight stories high, and phase 1 should complete by the end of 2010. It could likely be the greenest hospital in the United Kingdom. It has natural ventilation for the midseasons, a sedum green roof, combined heating and power, et cetera. At the same time, its façade optimizes daylight penetration. The design is rated 77 points with the BREEAM rating system.

Ulrich Dietz That's an extremely high value. That brings us right to our subject. You were one of the first architects to think "green." Do you regard yourself as a pioneer?

Ken Yeang I'm not sure. It's true that I have been thinking about the subject and working on green design far longer than most—since 1971, when I started work on my doctoral dissertation on ecological design and planning at Cambridge University.

Ulrich Dietz How did you come to make sustainability the center of your work so early on?

Ken Yeang I was a research assistant at Cambridge University working under Alex Pike and John Frazer on the Autonomous House project first mooted by Buckminster Fuller. A year before Pike died, he and Norman Foster designed the first house independent of all municipal utilities (water, electricity, sewerage, heating, etc.). I was so fascinated that after six months on the project I decided to devote my doctoral thesis to the theory of ecological design and planning. This became my life's agenda.

Ulrich Dietz Was the first ecological manifesto in architecture written at that time?

Ken Yeang None fully comprehensive at that time, although there were a few initial attempts. I am presently working on a version with some colleagues from Spain.

Ulrich Dietz But it was always your intention to make your theories reality as well?

Ken Yeang Yes. In 1974, my father had a stroke, and I flew back to the Far East to be with him. A year later, I started my architect's office in Kuala Lumpur joining my current business partner. Fortunately, my father got well again, but by that time I was entrenched in running my own architecture business.

Ulrich Dietz Was he also an architect?

Ken Yeang No, he was a medical doctor. He was a second-generation Chinese immigrant to Malaysia.

Ulrich Dietz What about your architecture is new? I understand it is based on the idea of "ecomimesis," as I read in one of your articles: the idea of imitating the properties and attributes of ecological systems?

Ken Yeang Yes and no. May I elucidate? My idea starts with General Systems Theory (GST), a concept developed by the Austrian biologist Ludwig von Bertalanffy. It is holistic and looks at systems in relation to their environment, regarding a system as more than the sum of its parts. From this as a framework, I developed my theory of ecodesign. It merges ecology with architecture. I observed how the natural environment and the human-made environment relate to each other and how they can be intertwined. My ecodesign approach is derived from that.

Ulrich Dietz So is biology your guiding discipline and not architecture?

Ken Yeang Precisely. I see biology as the beginning and end of everything. Nature is the greatest inventor of all time. It is my key source of inspiration.

Ulrich Dietz What does your ecodesign look like?

Ken Yeang Every building has to fit seamlessly and benignly into its natural environment; it should never be an isolated object. I always start by examining the physical conditions of a place, such as its ecology, topography, its climate, the groundwater and the whole hydrological balance, the flora and fauna, the bedrock and geology, et cetera. I try to integrate these natural aspects into the building design.

Ulrich Dietz Is nature your teacher?

Ken Yeang Yes. Before the industrial revolution, nature was more or less in equilibrium in which it was able to regenerate again and again. It is self-reactive. However, we as humans became excessively dominant over nature and have changed the biosphere radically, including effecting global climate change. The goal of ecodesign is to imitate stasis in nature. If we were to design our parks, our cities, and our buildings as artificial ecosystems, then these would operate integratively with the natural environment. For example, we should use the most renewable source of energy—the sun—and not nonrenewable energy resources such as fossil fuels. But I haven't yet mentioned nature's greatest quality.

Ulrich Dietz What's that?

Ken Yeang Nature wastes nothing. It reuses and recycles everything. One organism's waste becomes another's food. If we imitate this principle ecomimetically, we will no longer produce waste. All our emissions and products would be reused and reprocessed again and again and ultimately returned and reintegrated back into the natural environment. At the same time, energy and natural resources are used efficiently. That's what I mean by ecomimesis: imitating ecosystems by design. And that is, one of the key principles of my ecodesign strategies.

Ulrich Dietz Could you explain me the details of your ecological master planning?

Ken Yeang There are four strands of ecoinfrastructures: the green ecoinfrastructure, with its diverse flora and fauna that must be linked; the gray ecoinfrastructure of clean, carbon-neutral, low-energy technologies; the blue ecoinfrastructure being water/ aquatic systems and their management; and the red ecoinfrastructure of our human societies, our activities and lifestyles. The green ecoinfrastructure should dominate as the key infrastructure, so that human interventions will cause as little damage as possible. Do you know of the Dong Tang, the first carbon-neutral, emission-free city in the world?

Ulrich Dietz No. Where is it?

Ken Yeang Near Shanghai. The engineering firm ARUP designed it. They are great multidisciplinary engineers, and their design is exemplary—apart from one serious flaw. It has isolated patches of green but neither a continuous green ecological nexus nor green ecoinfrastructures linking the biotic constituents of the city and its urban development with the biome of its hinterland. The ecocity needs to restore and recreate self-sustaining natural habitats lost within the existing urban footprint by reintroducing flora, fauna and topographical features specific to the area. But an ecocity only regenerates itself if it is integrated with the local vegetation, since it alone is self-sustaining. Conventional green environments rely heavily on additives such as fertilizers, pesticides, fungicides, and insecticides. They are costly and detrimental to the environment. We have to protect the source, not just the outcomes, thus I believe in using nature's blueprint. All our major existent cities need to be retrofitted as ecocities and function as viable, natural habitats that function interdependently with nature.

Ulrich Dietz You believe Dong Tang will remain an artificial city?

Ken Yeang Without an ecological nexus and green ecoinfrastructure, it remains essentially clever engineering.

Ulrich Dietz Your green landmarks are primarily highrises. Why?

Ken Yeang I do not design just skyscrapers but actually all building types. The skyscrapers of the future should be located at transportation hubs. They are perhaps the most unecological of all built forms, since they use about thirty percent more energy and materials. So when we do build skyscrapers, they must be designed to be as sustainable as possible so that they destress urban conditions as much as possible.

Ulrich Dietz What building materials do you use?

Ken Yeang It depends on the project and its situation. We try to design for either long-life with high flexibility or for easy disassembly to facilitate recycling. Various materials have different environmental impacts (for example, steel versus concrete), different life cycles and levels of reuseabilities and embodied energy for their recycling. These are some of the factors in their selection.

Ulrich Dietz What does that mean?

Ken Yeang It could mean having mechanical bonding of materials as against chemical bonding to facilitate reuse. In any case, we need to have materials that enable the integrating of the biotic constituents continuously from the ground to the roof. In that sense, we are really more "vegitects" than architects! Our building design starts with bioclimatic responses; for example, we have designed wind-walls for mixed-mode natural ventilation, the use of "ecocells" to integrate vertically within the built structure, as a light-shaft that leads from the top of the built form to the lowest part to bring daylight, natural ventilation, rainwater harvesting, and vegetation into the inner parts of a building.

Ulrich Dietz One of your best known buildings is the EDITT Tower in Singapore. Can you tell me more about it?

Ken Yeang I tried to implement all my ideas of that time in it. We planted the vegetation between the various levels of the high-rise built form in a spiral ramp of biomass that weaves its way gently upward in the building. To use renewable sources of energy, we had photovoltaic panels on the east and west sides of the façade. To better harvest rainwater, we had a rainwater collector on the roof and scalloped-shaped sunshades to better harvest rainwater. The idea was to develop a human-made ecosystem in the built form of a tower.

 That sounds as exciting as the building looks! So one crucial aspect of the aesthetic of your architecture is having a precise analysis of the environment?

Ken Yeang Yes.

 Your exemplary master planning is one thing but the aesthetic outcome is another. How do you manage to create buildings that are both sustainable and look signature? Surely in your case the formula is no longer "form follows function"?

Ken Yeang No, perhaps more like "form follows nature as it changes over time." My aesthetic is the green aesthetic. But what should a green building look like? Certainly not modernist and pristine, but more like something fuzzy, hairy, and indeterminate. Just like nature—it might be amorphous, asymmetrical, polygonal, and sometimes crystalline.

 Your high-rises remind me of membranes.

Ken Yeang I like that. It's largely due to the filtering function of the façades that must breathe.

 And I like that! So for you, nature is the architect, and clearly all your buildings are prototypes. Do you still see yourself within any of the architectural traditions?

Ken Yeang Honestly, no. I don't belong to a particular "school of architecture." My approach is probably special because I operative passively. I do not so much compose a design but rather design integratively with the ecology of the place.

 The challenges you face are primarily ecological, geographic, and climatic. Do you plan differently depending on whether you are building in Germany or India?

Ken Yeang The basic principles are the same wherever, but we always try to bring the biological environment and the built environment into a balance, to bring nature back into urban spaces, and to design the entire built environment in a more organic way. That is applicable everywhere, including Germany.

 Do your green buildings cost more than traditional ones?

Ken Yeang The great thing is that the additional expenses are tiny compared to the outcomes. My deep green buildings can cost around six to seven percent more than the industry's cost standard for ecoarchitecture.

 How much do your buildings reduce energy use compared to conventional ones?

Ken Yeang An example: my sixteen-story, 98-meter-tall New National Library in Singapore is open twelve hours a day. Compared to office buildings of similar proportions, it uses around 172 kilowatt-hours per square meter per annum, rather than the usual 230 kilowatt-hours per square meter per annum in a typical office building. That's distinctly more energy-efficient. We achieve that by bioclimatic passive-mode design and by using low-energy systems and energy management systems.

 Is it easy for you to find clients?

Ken Yeang It's getting better. Gradually, more clients are beginning to understand my approach and to appreciate the inherent depth of my expertise.

 Can our planet survive without ecodesign and green architecture?

Ken Yeang Absolutely not. But we also need green governments, green cities, green industries, green food production, green economies with green products—a green lifestyle. Otherwise we have no hope for the future.

 Are you optimistic about our green future?

Ken Yeang Absolutely. I dream a green dream. But as Kermit the Frog in Sesame Street puts it so well: "It's not that easy being green." Still, we should all try to make the world as green as possible.

Thomas Alva Edison

"If we all did the things
we are capable of doing,
we would literally
astound ourselves."

"Someone has to do it." How often have I heard that sentence. The question is: Who is this someone? Interestingly, it is always the same people who then "do" it, who, as they say, "sort it out"—that is, address themes and arrange things. They are men and women who are discontent with things as they are and therefore develop solutions rather than just talk.

In olden times, they were pioneers who explored new worlds. My native region, Baden-Württemberg, also had such adventurers and travelers, scientists and inventors, writers and entrepreneurs. The most famous of them—the mathematician, astronomer, and philosopher of nature Johannes Kepler from Weil der Stadt—discovered the laws of the motion of the planets in 1606 and a little later the fundamentals of optics. In 1623, the astronomer and mathematician Wilhelm Schickard of Tübingen built the first calculating machine. Both were rebellious personalities, as was the writer, dramatist, philosopher, and historian Friedrich Schiller from Marbach am Neckar.

In the extensive literature by pioneers, I was impressed early on by the writings of the German naturalist Alexander von Humboldt, who in the early nineteenth century traveled through Latin America, the

United States, and Central Asia and thus was an intellectual forerunner to a globalized science. I also devoured a biography of the inventor and electrical engineer Nikola Tesla—the father of today's alternate current electrical supply, who was born in Smiljan, in the Croatian Military Frontier, in 1856. It described the life, but also the failures, of a forgotten genius who was unable to market his ideas, unlike the inventor-entrepreneur Thomas Edison, who was also a brilliant businessman.

After reading such books, I realized even in early youth that my future would not be that of a discoverer. So, as a rather mediocre student, I concentrated on at least doing well the sciences, and in my father's jewelry workshop in my home town I experimented with inventing new technical products. During school vacations I was also tutored by a retired engineer, who managed to teach me the connections between mathematics, physics, and technology in an intelligible and very fascinating way. It was a stroke of luck for me, for he triggered my passion to question ideas and things and to doubt apparently established facts, even when I studied engineering later.

That is how all pioneers begin, I believe. What also distinguishes them, both then and now, are curiosity and the courage for "creative destruction," the principle that the economist Joseph Schumpeter considered a prerequisite for economic and technological progress. New structures displace the old; creators have to destroy the existing. An even more crucial quality for pioneers is taking responsibility for one's own actions as well as for a community, an enterprise, and a society.

Pioneers take risks, whether physical or financial, and take responsibility even when they fail. In our society, in which everyone buys insurance for everything, this attitude seems to have gone out of fashion. The social market economy is in danger of becoming a preserve of the social state. And so workers in state institutions or large companies concentrate above all on not making mistakes in order to preserve their comfortable careers.

But only those who take risks, make mistakes, and are even permitted to fail without immediately losing their jobs will be able to develop the characteristics of a pioneer, from which the new will emerge. Being creative also means trying out things repeatedly on the model of trial and error; it can also mean wasting resources. That begins with basic development and ends with the marketing of new products. Failure is inevitable, since that is the only way to recognize how a new, correct path can be adopted.

This method of falsification was developed by the Austrian-British philosopher and theorist of science Karl Popper in his theory of critical rationalism. He described his attitude as "I may be wrong and you may be right, and by an effort we may get nearer to the truth."

In order to implement this fundamentally innovative insight, however, it would be necessary at school and later at the university and professionally to train together in trial and error, failure and responsibility. Then people would no longer prefer the most adaptable applicant but rather the independent-minded and socially competent one. The last of the great bankers, Siegmund Warburg—an entrepreneurial free spirit who should by all means serve as a role model again today—filtered applicants out by having their handwriting analyzed.

For several years now, enormous rates of growth have been observed in the economies of newly industrialized countries such as Brazil, Russia, India, and China. Countries that were only recently considered developing countries have become locomotives of global growth in just a short time. The causes for this are, on the one hand, enormous domestic markets but also, on the other, the fact that China and India in particular became global production facilities and service centers.

They developed enormous capacity for many industrially produced products and easily outsourced services, and Western countries in particular as sites for cheap production.

Moreover, these countries have millions of people who found companies because they recognize the opportunities for a globally networked economy. They are men and women who want to achieve something, who are prepared to achieve a great deal with a prospect for rapid economic success. They create products and come up with ideas for services in very short cycles. One of these new pioneers is Shiv Nadar, founder and Chairman of the Board of HCL Technologies, a technology services company that operates worldwide from its base in India. When Nadar and some friends founded his company in 1976, most people thought he had no chance. Today 60,000 employees in twenty-six countries have earnings of five billion dollars.

To him as to everyone else who wants to be a pioneer, the words of the American writer Mark Twain apply: "The man with a new idea is a crank until the idea succeeds."

Johann Wolfgang von Goethe

"To new shores beckons
me a new-born day."

Not everyone approaches the new with as light a heart as Germany's great poet. But we hope that this book has stimulated your desire to test your own ability to innovate. All you need is an adequate portion of curiosity and the insight that the new cannot be planned but can only be sought. It does not belong to an existing canon of rules, and when it creates a new one, it must, if it wishes to remain new, also destroy it or at least change it again over the course of time. So dare to venture into unfamiliar terrain, try out, experiment, mix the familiar and the foreign, and discover how innovative you are!

Here are the ultimate tips, the trump cards, as it were, of our conversation partners, who play them in the infinite game with the new:

· Believe in yourself—the secret of charisma
· Trust your own ideas—especially when others consider them weird
· Learn to love dreams
· Think in every which way
· Do something rather than letting things be
· Dare to cross boundaries
· Shift your point of view and perspectives
· Preserve your roots in order to create new things from them

· Use information
· Be persistent and hardworking
· Trust your inspiration and intuition
· Learn to love the unfamiliar
· Permit creativity
· Concentrate on the essential
· Take responsibility
· Learn to view nature as an inventor
· Allow emotions
· Do not shy away from resistance
· Admit mistakes
· Have the courage to fail…
· …but never relinquish
· And never lose your sense of humor.

Because: It always turns out better than you think!

Like most of the projects and activities described here, this book is the result of outstanding teamwork. Many people participated with enthusiasm and commitment.

I wish to thank first my conversation partners, who shared with me their insatiable passion for the new in intense discussions under inspiring and friendly circumstances. Everywhere I was received with open arms and great congeniality. Each conversation provided me with further insights into what the pioneer spirit is, into the attractive power that the magic of the new exerts, and how it repeatedly makes trailblazing innovations possible.

My sincere gratitude also goes out to the team that accompanied me: the journalist and author Dr. Eva Karcher, who moderated the interviews and carried them out with me, and photographer Michael Dannenmann, who documented our encounters in wonderful photographs. Together we crisscrossed the world, intensely working but remaining in good spirits, despite the occasional time pressures, and we had a lot of fun in the process.

I would also like to thank my publisher, Christian Boros, who founded the DISTANZ Verlag in parallel with working on this book, and now

The new *New* will be one of its first publications. Our conversations about the new in art and on literature and aesthetics were also stimulating and fascinating. My sincere thanks are also owed to his copublisher, Uta Grosenick, for her valuable suggestions during the development process. I am grateful to the graphic designer Mathias-Kim Beyer of the Agentur Boros for his patience as he implemented countless design proposals until we found the right one. The translators, Steven Lindberg, Tom Morrison, and Michael Turnbull, and the editor, Sabine Bleßmann, who spent many an hour editing the texts and giving them their final polish, also deserve my sincere thanks.

My coworkers on the GFT team have also earned my profound thanks, in particular Fanny Marschner, who directed the research work and always kept a tight rein on the coordination of the project and the interviews, as well as Andrea Wlcek and Christina Vontin, who supported us with valuable tips. My gratitude also goes out to my colleagues Marika Lulay and Dr. Jochen Ruetz, who covered my back in my day-to-day business so I could spend the time necessary. I am also grateful to all my other colleagues at GFT Technologies AG, who got involved in various research tasks.

My gratitude also goes out to numerous discussion partners and good friends who accompanied us: Dr. Markus Kerber, Dr. Frank Obergfell, Dr. Johannes Probst, Hans-Willi Schondelmaier, and Martin Veit. They were also inspiring sparring partners and helpful advisers.

Finally, special gratitude is owed to my family, who offered me encouragement and love during the long work on this project. My wife, Maria, and my sons, Florenz and Lukas, always stood by me and showed great understanding for the seemingly endless hours when I was sitting at my writing desk or disappeared traveling. Maria advised me in many circumstances with equal measures of warmth and critical engagement. Her profound remarks and recommendations were always spot-on and indispensable. I cannot thank her enough for that.

<u>Ulrich Dietz</u>

The entrepreneurial spirit flows in his blood. Born in Pforzheim in 1958 to a jewelry manufacturer, Ulrich Dietz was nineteen when he founded his first company, which produced technical drawings. In Reutlingen and Furtwangen he studied mechanical engineering and product engineering and after receiving his degree he cofounded the Transferzentrum für Informationstechnologie (Transfer center for information technology) of the Steinbeis-Stiftung für Wirtschafts-förderung. In 1987 he and a partner cofounded the information technology company GFT in St. Georgen in the Black Forest, and as its managing director he took the company public in 1999. GFT Technologies AG now has about 1,200 employees and is one of the leading information technology service providers in the financial sector. GFT conceives and implements IT solutions and places engineers and computer specialists worldwide. As a board member of BITKOM, the large European IT association, Ulrich Dietz also addresses the concerns of the IT business in Germany and supports Germany as a site for innovation. Since 2010 he has been teaching entrepreneurship at the Universität Stuttgart-Hohenheim.

<u>Eva Karcher</u>

She owes her profession to her curiosity. Born in Heidelberg in 1960, Eva Karcher studied art history, philosophy, and history and trained as a dancer at the same time. After receiving her PhD with a dissertation on the New Objectivity painter Otto Dix, she worked first in galleries, publishing houses, and as a critic for the *Süddeutsche Zeitung*. That was followed by eight years as arts editor for Burda Verlag and Gruner + Jahr. In 1997 she became a freelance journalist, author, and expert on the art market. She has become internationally known for her essays, reportage, portraits, and analyses of the art market as well as big interviews of famous personalities from the art and creative scene for the *Süddeutsche Zeitung* and *Vogue,* for which she works regularly. She also conceives and realizes books, most recently *Prototypes* published by DuMont in Cologne in 2009.

He sees portrait photography as an opportunity to get closer to people and their essences through images. Michael Dannenmann, born in Stuttgart in 1959, studied painting and photography at the Kunstakademie Stuttgart and the Fachhochschule Dortmund. In 1990 he opened his studio in Düsseldorf, which has established an international reputation. Dannenmann manages to take photographs of highly characteristic sensitivity, in which those portrayed recognize themselves and at the same time discover a new perspective. He has photographed numerous stars, including Bill Gates, Dennis Hopper, Michael Schumacher, Phil Collins, Patricia Kaas, and Isabella Rossellini.

Ansari, Anousheh: *My Dream of Stars: From Daughter of Iran to Space Pioneer,* Palgrave Macmillan: New York 2010

Beise, Marc, Ulrich Schäfer (Ed.), *Wirtschaftskrisenwunder— Wo der Aufschwung herkommt,* Süddeutsche Zeitung Wirtschaft: München 2010

Bernstein, Josh: *Digging for the truth: One Man's Epic Adventure Exploring the World's Greatest Archaeological Mysteries,* Gotham: New York 2006

Bhidé, Amar: *A Call for Judgment: Sensible Finance for a Dynamic Economy,* Oxford University Press: Oxford 2010

---: *The Venturesome Economy: How Innovation Sustains Prosperity in a More Connected World,* Princeton University Press: Princeton 2008

---: *The Origin and Evolution of New Businesses,* Oxford University Press: Oxford 2000

---: *Of Politics and Economic Reality: The Art of Winning Elections with Sound Economic Policies,* Basic Books: New York 1984

Bröckling, Ulrich: *Das unternehmerische Selbst: Soziologie einer Subjektivierungsform,* Suhrkamp: Berlin 2007

Cube, Felix von: *Lust an Leistung: die Naturgesetze der Führung,* Piper: München 2000

---: *Fordern statt Verwöhnen: die Erkenntnisse der Verhaltensbiologie in Erziehung und Führung,* Piper: München 1997

Fry, Stephen: "The iPad Launch: Can Steve Jobs Do It Again?" *Time Magazin,* 1st April 2010, http://www.time.com/time/business/article/0,8599,1976935,00.html (12.4.2010)

Groys, Boris: *Über das Neue. Versuch einer Kulturökonomie,* Fischer Verlag: Frankfurt 2004

Günak, Murat: Taramor: Eine Weihnachtsgeschichte, s. l.: 2008

Hennecke, *Hans Jörg: Friedrich August von Hayek zur Einführung,* Junius Verlag: Hamburg 2008

Heuser, Uwe Jean: *Schöpfer und Zerstörer: große Unternehmer und ihre Momente der Entscheidung,* Rowohlt: Hamburg 2004

Horx, Matthias: *Das Buch des Wandels. Wie Menschen Zukunft gestalten,* Deutsche Verlagsanstalt: München 2009

---: *Wie wir leben werden: Unsere Zukunft beginnt jetzt,* Campus Verlag: München 2005

Kelley, Tom: *The Art of Innovation: Success Through Innovation,* Profile Business: London 2002

Kuhn, Thomas S., Lorenz Krüger and Hermann Vetter: *Die Entstehung des Neuen: Studien zur Struktur der Wissenschaftsgeschichte,* Suhrkamp: Frankfurt 1987

Leibinger, Berthold: *Es sind die geistigen Kräfte die die Welt verändern: Reden,* Leibinger: Ditzingen 2002

Lewis, Michael: *The New New Thing: A Silicon Valley Story,* Penguin: London 2000

Llosa, Claudia (Dir.): *Madeinusa,* 2006, DVD, Cameo media: 2010

---: *The Milk of Sorrow,* 2009

Lotter, Wolf: *Die kreative Revolution. Was kommt nach dem Industriekapitalismus?* Murmann Verlag, Hamburg 2009

Mutius, Bernhard von: *Die andere Intelligenz—Wie wir morgen denken werden,* Klett-Cotta: Stuttgart 2008

---: *Die Verwandlung der Welt. Ein Dialog mit der Zukunft.* Klett-Cotta: Stuttgart 2000

Neiman, Susan: *Moral Clarity: A Guide for Grown-Up Idealists,* Princeton University Press: Princeton 2009

---: *Evil in Modern Thought: An Alternative History of Thinking,* Princeton University Press: Princeton 2002

Opaschowski, Horst W.: *Deutschland 2030: Wie wir in Zukunft leben werden,* Gütersloher Verlagshaus: Gütersloh 2008

Parra, Hèctor, Lisa Randall: *Hypermusic prologue: a projective opera in seven planes,* CD, Kairos: Vienna 2010

Peters, Tom: *The Circle of Innovation: You Can't Shrink Your Way to Greatness,* Knopf, New York 1997

Pierer, Heinrich von, Bolko von Oetinger: *Wie kommt das Neue in die Welt,* Hanser: München 1997

Popper, Karl R.: *All Life is Problem Solving,* Routledge: London 2001

---: *In Search of a Better World: Lectures and Essays from Thirty Years,* Routledge: London 1995

Prahalad, C. K., M. S. Krishnan: *The New Age of Innovation: Driving Cocreated Value Through Global Networks,* McGraw-Hill: New York 2008

Randall, Lisa: *Warped Passages: Unravelling the Universe's Hidden Dimensions,* Penguin: London 2006

Scholtissek, Stephan: *Die Magie der Innovation: Erfolgsgeschichten von Audi bis Zara,* mi-Wirtschaftsbuch: München 2009

Schumpeter, Joseph A.: *Capitalism, Socialism and Democracy,* Routledge: London 2010

Seele, Peter (Ed.): *Philosophie des Neuen,* Wissenschaftliche Buchgesellschaft: Darmstadt 2008

Yeang, Ken: Ecodesign: *A Manual for Ecological Design,* John Wiley & Sons: London 2008

Imprint

Editor
Ulrich Dietz

Author
Dr. Eva Karcher

Photographer
Michael Dannenmann

Project Management
Fanny Marschner

Editorial Office
Sabine Bleßmann

Translations
Steven Lindberg
pp. 68ff., 86ff.: Tom Morrison
pp. 110ff., 142ff., 152ff.: Michael Turnbull

Design
BOROS, Mathias-Kim Beyer

Production Management
Nicole Rankers

Production
Kessler Druck + Medien, Bobingen

© Photo p. 202: Elias Hassos

© 2010 DISTANZ Verlag GmbH
All rights reserved.

Distribution
GESTALTEN, Berlin
www.gestalten.com
sales@gestalten.com

ISBN 978-3-942405-09-6
Printed in Germany

Published by
DISTANZ Verlag, Berlin
www.distanz.de